6th April 89

Henry P. Chalk

THE DEVIL SITS AMONG THE CONGREGATION

This story is about two young teenagers, a boy and a girl. They had an aunt who was intent on getting her hands on the family business. She started to cause trouble by setting false tales and rumours about; they mainly concerned the two teenagers.

See how they dealt with this, and have a good laugh at the hilarious tactics used by this young man.

This story has been written for people of all ages. It is not as religious as its title suggests. I hope you enjoy it.

H. C.

THE DEVIL SITS AMONG THE CONGREGATION

H. Chalk

ARTHUR H. STOCKWELL LTD.
Elms Court   Ilfracombe
Devon

ISBN 0 7223 2221-6

Printed in Great Britain by
Arthur H. Stockwell Ltd.
Elms Court   Ilfracombe
Devon

CONTENTS

The find

CHAPTER 1

Kathleen was a sweet young lady in her fourteenth year. She was a slim built girl, not very well-dressed and obviously not well-fed. But despite this she was quite a pretty girl, originating from the North of England. She tended to be quite a loner, not joining in very much with the girls of her age and was often seen looking after the younger children in the playground of the school in the small town of Portstanton where she now lived.

If you could have cast your eye around the playground in those days a young man soon to leave school could also be seen. He was usually writing notes or the like in a note pad or book. Occasionally he would cast his eye around the playground until he could see Kathleen; he would gaze at her for a moment then back to his writing. His name was Tom Monkton, he was about five foot six inches tall, and quite a strong looking lad with a serious look on his face. He also, like Kathleen, had a rather reserved manner about him. His hobby was writing and his one ambition in life so far was to become a novelist. His mother was an ex-Dutch servant girl who had married his father back in 1916. She taught Tom to speak the Dutch language quite well. He wanted to travel if possible to try and give himself inspiration for his writings; settling down to a job of work was far from his thoughts just now. He would get his pocket-money by working as a caddie on the local golf course. Owing to his pleasant manner and his obliging way, he became a great favourite among the golfers as a caddie. Some, when arriving at the club to play a round of golf, would call his name to see if he was there to caddie for them.

Some weeks during his school holidays he would earn almost as much as his father who was a jobbing builder in the town. But above all Tom seemed to be attracted to this little lady named Kathleen.

She led a rather hard life; her father had died from war wounds a

9

few years after the war; now her mother had to take to a wheelchair and was told that she would eventually become bedridden. Kathy was an only child so her burden was great for one so young.

During the lunch hours on school-days, Tom, who owned an old bike would loan it to her to ride home to attend to her mother's needs. She never seemed to have time for going out with other girls of her age, such as going to the local cinema, or to go for a walk on Sunday afternoons; instead she devoted her time to her mother. The only regular outing for her was to fetch medicine from the doctor's surgery, or to go to the little Methodist Church near where she lived for Sunday evening service. Money was very scarce in her house, the only income being a widow's pension plus a little extra, because her husband had died from war wounds, arranged for her by the British Legion. This fact of course shows why little Kathy was poorly dressed and a bit undernourished.

One evening the local Methodist minister called on Tom's parents. As he was about to leave he turned to Tom who was sat there writing and said, "By the way young man I feel that I must thank you from the bottom of my heart for the way in which you have helped young Kathy."

"Hello!" exclaimed Tom's mother teasingly. "What's this I hear?"

The minister then proceeded to explain to Tom's parents more fully how Tom had helped the Eccles family in their time of need, as he realized that they had become quite interested and seemed to know very little about it. They heard how Tom had lent Kathy his old bike at lunch-times; how he had dug and planted her garden, and had kept them supplied with firewood; plus doing many other jobs for them.

Tom's mother was the first to speak. She said, "But isn't her sister there?" Meaning Kathy's aunt.

"She was," replied Pastor Jones, "but she had to go home suddenly because her husband was injured in the coal mines."

"Oh dear!" said Tom's mother. "Don't any of their neighbours help at all?"

"Very little unfortunately," replied Pastor Jones.

There was silence for a moment.

"Oh Lord please forgive us" explained Tom's mother. "I'll go round now, tonight."

'I wonder what I can take to help,' she pondered.

"You could try a hot fish and chip supper for a start" suggested Tommy. "They can't even afford such luxury that's for sure."

"What a nice idea" replied father, who had been listening intently. "I shall call at the fish bar, then I'll meet you at the house. What number was it again?" asked father.

"Number six Rowleys Estate" replied Tom.

As he put his jacket on father remarked, "I must say very well done to that most thoughtful son of mine; very Christian" he commented. Then he dashed off for the fish suppers.

Mother put some things in a basket, odd things she thought might help Kathy and her mum; then she left with Pastor Jones for number six Rowleys.

Tommy continued with his writings; about two hours later mother and father returned.

"Kettle's boiling Mum," called Tom, as he packed up his things from the kitchen table.

"Lovely" she replied. "We came home via the chippies, so it's fish and chips for quickness tonight."

"Come on Tom, it's your big favourite, cod" said father.

"In that case I'm with you" replied Tom, as he took his place at the table. "I could eat a boiled whale tonight" he said.

"Never tried it son" replied father causing a laugh.

"Now then you two stop larking about" said mother as the Monkton family settled down to their supper.

The talking point was of course the Eccles family.

Tom's mother said "What intrigues me is how did you come to be helping Kathy in the first place?"

"That's easy" replied Tom, "she used to be always crying; then one day I could stand it no longer, so I took her to one side and asked her what the heck was wrong. I said things like 'Who has upset you?' She was sobbing so much she couldn't tell me at first, then she blurted it all out. She said the doctor had told her aunt that her mother would never get any better; she could only get worse. 'Now you listen to me my girl, you might as well know the truth your father is dead, therefore you will have to go into a home as well as your mother. I can't have you up North with me because we are full up already.' Having said that her aunt set off on her return trip up North leaving Kathy heartbroken."

"Oh poor little darling" said Tom's mother. "How cruel her aunt is."

"Yes Kathy detests her aunt" replied Tom.

"How did you stop her crying then?" asked father.

"Well I made her tell me everything, the lot," said Tom, "and she did; no one else to talk to I suppose."

Tom fell silent now until his mother prompted him by saying, "Something else must have happened. What did you do then?"

"Well," replied Tom, "I never told you two for a start, because mother has always told me not to go round with girls. But in order to help as help I had to, I offered to lend her my bike to pop home at midday. This I thought would help her to sort out her mother's needs. She could help her mum provided she had the time; that's where my bike came in, it saved her travelling time. She could hardly ride when she started borrowing it but she's very good and confident now. Then one Sunday I saw my chance, so I asked Pastor Jones for some advice, because I thought I wouldn't get it from you."

Mother started to speak, but Tom put his hand up saying, "Please hear me out now. Pastor Jones suggested a plan. *Firstly*, he said, 'Get the nurse to call; she's a good regular Methodist, she will know just what to do.' *Secondly*, 'Get the nurse to talk to Kathy's mother to see if she will agree to let Kathy come to Church with you, that way she will know where Kathy is, it could give Kathy more faith to cope with life.' *Thirdly*, he said, 'I have a friend down at Brighton, he is a specialist in her type of illness. I'll have a chat with him, he might be able to come up with something and I'll let you know what he works out.' That mother, is how I got involved, I suppose you could say I couldn't mind my own business."

"No. No," exclaimed mother and father together, "we are both very proud of you lad, very proud indeed a good Christian act on your part."

"I think looking at it now that God was using you to help her" added mother, and she continued "I'm really going to help Kathy after being with her tonight. I've decided her heart is in the right place alright."

"And no mistake" agreed father.

"Then neither of you will call me a cissy over this?" asked Tom.

"No, certainly not indeed, we both like what you did" said mother. "I only wish that we had found out sooner. You see Tom, her dad gave his life for his country, our country. Now your father and I won't stand by and see her put on. We are going to work out a plan tonight, like you and Pastor Jones did. She'll be OK, you'll see."

"By the way" said father, I do agree son, she certainly is a pretty little gal, don't you think so Mother?"

"I agree," said mother laughing. "By the time we've finished with her she won't be just pretty, she'll be absolutely lovely, you'll see."

Tom blushed crimson excusing himself by saying "Now I must get ready for the morning."

Next day was a school day, Friday in fact. Kathy told Tom how his mum and dad had called; how his dad had brought some real gorgeous freshly cooked fish and chips; how he sat talking to her mum while she ate her supper.

"Funny thing Tom, both our dads served in the same regiment. Your mum helped me do some washing and ironing, then we made some cakes — jam tarts, and a few mince pies so that I could take some to school."

"Well," replied Tom "if Pastor Jones hadn't mentioned it they would never have known."

"Known what?" asked Kathy, munching a mince pie rather hungrily.

"Well about all your troubles" replied Tom.

"Oh of course" she replied. "But I do like your mum, she's so kind, she seems to understand. She's a bit foreign or something isn't she Tom?"

"You could say that I suppose" replied Tom. "She's Dutch, that's why she was able to teach me Dutch, it could be useful later on, who knows?"

The next day being Saturday, Tom set off early to hoe through Kathy's garden to try and keep the weeds down. After this he went to the golf club telling Kathy that he had a job to go to. She smiled at this knowing what he meant.

He hadn't left the house long, when his mum came to see Kathy and her mother. Mrs Monkton, that's Tom's mother of course, obtained permission from Kathy's mother to take her out to the shops with her, which was almost a mile away. Off they went to catch the bus on the corner which took them down to the bus depot in the town. They had finished their shopping and were nearing the bus depot in the town when Mr Monkton came along in his van.

He stopped and shouted "Can I help you ladies?"

The parcels and bags were loaded up, then with the passengers inside, off they went.

As they carried the shopping into number six, Kathy noticed, standing by the back door, a very nice lady's bicycle. Eventually Mrs Monkton came out to show her the bike.

"Now" she said, "this is your bike Kathy, you see it's really my old bike, now I don't need it anymore, so I've had it looked over and any repairs needed have been done. If you will just sit on I'll get my husband to alter the saddle for you." She sat on; the saddle needed to go down a bit. Kathy saw that it had a carrier and a front basket, it even had a new dress-guard.

"But Mrs Monkton," protested Kathy, "I can't buy it, I haven't any money."

"No dear, I'm giving it to you, I don't need it anymore, so rather than let it rust out I'm giving it to you. I thought how handy it could be for you going to the shops, the school, and the doctors, in fact anywhere you have to go. Please take it Kathy with all my love."

Poor little Kathy she looked at the bike, it looked so beautiful. Slowly her eyes filled with tears, she just threw herself into Mrs Monkton's arms. This beautiful bike with its green markings was really hers. She had never been shown such kindness, she just sobbed her heart out with her uncontrolled happiness.

"It's alright Kathy, we know that you have had a very hard time of it indeed, but we really are your friends you know, and we shall stand by you always so please don't be afraid anymore." She held Kathy gently until she had finished crying.

"I'm sorry I lost control of myself Mrs Monkton, really I am. You won't tell mum will you?"

"Of course I won't dear."

"Oh, and please don't tell Tom he doesn't like it if I cry."

"I won't tell anyone Kathy dear. We'll just keep it a secret, you know I'm really very pleased with Master Thomas he's quite grown up you know" said Mrs Monkton laughing now.

"Yes" replied Kathy "and he's quite strong as well. He can dig without stopping for ever such a long time, and he's very quick to stand up for me over nothing — he does sometimes."

"I know what you mean dear" replied Mrs Monkton.

"Hello!" she said "here's Pastor Jones, with another man, I wonder what they want?"

The two men came along to the back door to greet the ladies.

"Now," said Pastor Jones, "this is Doctor Harrington. The thing is Kathy he would like to examine your mother; you see he is a specialist in her type of ailment. He has seen your own doctor and he has given his permission for him to examine your mother. You see Kathy there may be a cure."

"Oh I see" replied Kathy. "I'll just pop in and warn her." After awhile Kathy came back saying "She's ready sir and if you need a woman in there could Mrs Monkton help, as the nurse has already left?"

"Everyone went into the kitchen as Mrs Eccles was in bed in the sitting-room. Doctor Harrington went in, after about twenty minutes he came out.

"Now" he said. "I have examined Mrs Eccles. I am almost sure that I can operate successfully, but unfortunately she will have to come down to Brighton where I will carry out further investigations. Now, if my theory is correct I will operate and it should be quite successful."

"You mean sir, my mum could walk again?"

"Yes, and run if she feels like it."

Little Kathy just cried with joy. Mrs Monkton lent her a handkerchief and gave her a cuddle, while the doctor explained that it could take up to twelve weeks. He carefully put away his notes into his case, "I shall let Pastor Jones know as soon as I have a vacant bed, within about ten days I would think. I'll bid you goodbye now ladies" he said, shaking hands with them. Then he left with Pastor Jones.

"Oh Mrs Monkton, do you think he can?" asked Kathy looking up with her eyes full of tears of happiness.

"Seems like there is a good chance dear replied Mrs Monkton. Look I'll put the kettle on for you, while you go and see your mum. By that time we'll have a pot of tea made. I expect your mum could do with one. Now we must pray hard for success" said Mrs Monkton, as Kathy ran in to see her mother.

When Kathy came out she was all smiles, she said that the doctor had told mum that he believed it was a cyst pressing on the base of her spine. He couldn't be more certain until he had her in hospital to prove his diagnosis; then after he has removed it she should be quite normal. Kathy explained to Mrs Monkton, that her mum wanted to go, but was rather worried about what would become of her.

"Can I see your mum Kathy?" asked Mrs Monkton.

"Oh, yes just go in."

Kathy poured herself a cup of tea and had a large slice of cake while Mrs Monkton had a chat with her mother.

"Now my dear" said Mrs Monkton, "I understand that you can have treatment, now please don't worry about Kathy she can come to us. I have a lovely spare room for her, and she will be well looked after, then hopefully all will soon be well, and please always remember that we are your Christian friends my dear."

"And I thank God for that" replied Mrs Eccles, "but I'm still worried about the cost of it all."

"We shall see to the bills as they arrive, now no more worrying" said Mrs Monkton, "I absolutely forbid it. I must go now or I won't have anything ready for those two men of mine; young Thomas can eat as much as his father you know."

"I expect he can" replied Mrs Eccles. He's a fine young man and no mistake — I like him very much."

"Well I must go now, anything you want just send Kathy round to me on her bike." Then she shouted 'goodbye' to Kathy and left.

Mr Monkton came in for his midday meal, but no Tom.

"I wonder what he's up to?" said mother.

"Golf course again I suppose" replied father.

"Oh well, I'll just keep his hot, he'll be here soon. He'll never go without his food for long that's dead certain."

It was just before two o'clock when Master Thomas came running in.

"Sorry I'm late" he said, "only I found some silver and gold goblets and things." Then he rushed off to wash his hands.

As he came back his mother put his lunch on the table before him. "It might be a bit scrumped up but that's your fault Thomas."

"Yeah" he agreed, "couldn't help it could I, because I had to go down to the police station: I ran all the way home from there, now I've got to go right over to the golf course to get my bike." Then he ate his meal ravenously. "Coo, I was hungry" he said.

"Now" said father, "why don't you start at the beginning and tell me how you got mixed up with the police?"

"Well," replied Tom, "I was caddying for Chief Superintendent Everit from the police station, I always caddy for him you see; when we got round to the place we call Holly Bush Corner he lost his ball in the thick holly growth; we were both in there looking for it when I saw two big sacks, they were tied at the top with a necktie. I was nosey I suppose, so I opened one; it was full of silver and gold cups and things, so I called the superintendent over. He came saying, 'What's to do Tommy lad?' So I said, 'I wonder who dumped all this rubbish, only it looks quite nice to me.' I had taken one out, he had a look, then he said 'Come back out Tommy.' We came out of the bushes, then he scribbled a note and said 'Run like hell Tommy, take this to the clubhouse and give it to Major Jopling, the Club Secretary. He will phone the police. You stay there until they arrive, then bring them up here to me. I shall wait here. They will arrive by car so guide them up here. Do you understand?' 'Yes' I replied, 'I've got it.' 'Right now, run for it Tommy, if it's what I think it is, there will be a fat reward.' So I ran like a bat out of hell."

"Thomas," said his mother sharply, "you mustn't say that, it's not nice."

"Oh sorry, I forgot in my old age. Anyway I found Major Jopling, he was cleaning his car out in front of the clubhouse. He took me inside, got on the phone, and the police arrived within minutes. I got in the car, there was a policeman and a civilian; he seemed to be the boss.''

"He'll be a CID man" said father, "go on.''

So Tommy told how he guided the car up across the golf links to the superintendent; then how the police searched the whole area.

"They took the sacks and we all went to the police station. Then I had to write a statement saying how I found them, because the 'Super' said if I didn't write a statement I couldn't legally claim any reward. Then he read and signed my statement himself. Tommy he said, 'You can write better than my coppers; it's neat, tidy and very smart.' I can't say for sure mind but I believe the loot was stolen from Lord Challenor, he lives in that big Manor House about a mile further on, you know up that long front drive.''

"I know where you mean" agreed father. "So you've had quite a day so far then. I can run you over for your bike now, if you like, only I think mother and Kathy have got some news for you as well.''

"I'll go with you now," replied Tom, "because you must be going back to work. I'll get my bike, then I'll come back to Mum and Kathy.''

Tommy came home on his bike to find his mother and Kathy getting ready to do some baking. Kathy announced that she was going to learn how to make Dutch apple cake.

"Coo, that's smashing" agreed Tom.

Mother had the fire going really well and was washing her hands ready for cooking.

"I believe" said Tommy, "that you have both got some news to tell me.''

"Oh yes, you don't know" replied Kathy.

While she sat at the table chopping up apples, she explained to Tommy what the doctor had said. She stopped every now and then to smack Tommy's hand for stealing pieces of apples and popping them in his mouth.

Soon the baking was underway and the lovely smell of fresh cakes filled the house.

Tommy had left the kitchen for a while to write about finding the stolen silver on the golf course. While out in the kitchen, oh boy, there was golden Dutch apple cake, fruit cake, and lots of rock cakes. Now the final baking was going into the oven, a batch of lovely looking pasties and sausage rolls.

Kathy would take home her basket full for tea and for the following day.

With all the work done now they sat chatting over a cup of tea.

"I saw you having trouble with Tommy," said Mrs Monkton.

"Yes, he was pinching pieces of apple you see, so I smacked his hand."

"He's very mischievous like that dear, and by the way, why don't you just call me Auntie Getchen, or just plain Auntie. It would be much more friendly, don't you think?"

"Can I?" asked Kathy, blowing at the hot rock cake she was eating. I don't know anyone with a name like 'Gretchen' " she mused. "Nice though."

"Well you see dear it's Dutch, I was born in Holland."

"How did you get over here then?" asked Kathy.

"Well I will tell you — I was brought up in an orphanage, then when I was about your age, nearly fourteen years old, I was asked if I would like to go out to service, working a big house. I didn't know what this meant, so I said 'Can I try it?' There was an English family living near there; the husband was a diplomat from the Foreign Office. They had one child, a daughter of eight, and they employed a daily help woman. I was to live in. I spent three happy years working for them, then they had to come home. They took a house at Worthing, and they asked me if I would like to go to England with them. Well I had no relations anywhere in Holland, I liked the family very much, also I could by that time speak English fairly well. I agreed to stay with them, so we all came over to live at Worthing. Then the war broke out. One day I was out shopping for the lady of the house when my shopping bag broke, my shopping went all over the road. Now passing at that time was a smart young soldier, he saw what happened and rushed to help me. He went into a shop and came out with two carrier bags, then he helped me to gather up my things, and you know who it was don't you dear?"

"No not really Auntie Gretchen" replied Kathy.

"Well I'll tell you, it was Tom's father."

"Oh Auntie!" she screamed suddenly. "Did you marry him?"

"Eventually I did. He was very nice to me and so kind. On my evenings off we would go to the cinema, and then we would walk back to where I lived and worked. I was allowed to bring him in for a cup of tea before he went back to his camp. Then one day he had to leave for the front line. When he came home we were married. Eventually the war ended, and he was discharged from the army. Then he came home and took over his father's business and we've been living here ever since."

"Oh Auntie, it was a lovely, lovely, story, I did enjoy it. I'm so pleased that I came to help with the baking. I really have learned something new today. Thank you so much Auntie."

As auntie started to wash up the cooking utensils, someone

knocked at the front door.

"See who that is for me Kathy my hands are wet."

Kathy straightened up her apron and ran to open the door.

A gentleman stood there, he took off his hat and said "I'm looking for a young man called Tommy Monkton, my dear."

"Yes Sir, he's here" replied Kathy, "I'll call him."

Kathy went to call Tom, who came running. Tom's mother had dried her hands and was also coming now.

"I'm Lord Challenor" he said as Tom's mother came to the door, "and you would be Mr Thomas Monkton I presume young man?"

"Correct sir," answered Tom.

"Well now young man, I have come to see you because you have earned a reward that I have had on offer. It's for anyone who should find or give information leading to the return of my family's gold and silver plate; and that young man according to the superintendent of the police is you."

"Please come in Sir" invited Mrs Monkton.

His lordship followed her into the sitting-room and made himself comfortable.

"Now young man, I have a cheque here for £100 which is the reward offered by me. I will put your name on it so." He wrote on the cheque and dated it, then handing it to Tom he said "May I ask what you will do with it?"

"I shall bank it" replied Tom. "But I really do need a portable typewriter."

"That's a strange thing for a young man like you to want" he replied.

"Yes sir, you see I'm thinking of becoming a writer, and I'm hoping one day to become a novelist."

"Well, well," exclaimed his lordship, "so you like writing?"

"Love it sir," replied Tom. "I was writing when you came about how I came across your stolen silver."

"Were you indeed," replied his lordship smiling. "Could I read it do you think?" he asked.

"Yes Sir," agreed Tom, pulling out his note pad.

The pad was handed over to his lordship who read the article.

"Bless my soul! this is very good indeed. How old are you Thomas?"

"Well I have exactly one week to do at school sir, then I'm finished. I'm fourteen years old you see."

"Well now Thomas, what would you say if I offered you a job on my newspaper as a trainee reporter?" said his lordship.

Tom was considering this and his lordship was watching his face.

"You know where my offices are" he continued. "Half-way up the High Street. Now this little job should give you some experience and no mistake. You see reading this article that you have just written I would say even now that my chaps aren't capable of such modern work. This my son is quite outstanding considering your age. Now what do you say? Shall I give you more time to think about it?"

"No sir," replied Tom. "I'll take the job."

"Wonderful! Then I shall call you Thomas. Can I print this report that you have just written?"

"If you think it's good enough" replied Tom.

"May I suggest something Thomas," said his lordship. "Can you come with me now, then I can introduce you to the reporter that you will be training under. He can show you around the works and show you the office."

Tommy ran for his coat, then off he went in the big black Rolls with his lordship.

On arrival at the printing works they went into a neatly laid out office, and a lady secretary was sent to find a certain reporter. At last the man came into the office, he was an oldish man and apparently soon to retire.

"Arnold" said his lordship, "I want you to meet Thomas."

They shook hands.

"Now before I say another word Arnold read this, and see how much it has to be altered before the editor receives it."

Arnold read it, looked at his lordship, looked back at the report, looked at his lordship again, then said, "Nothing to alter sir."

"Exactly, that's what I thought" replied his lordship. "Effie, take this through to the editor for me. Now you two, well I really need to explain to you Arnold."

Then his lordship told him about Thomas and his find of the silver, and how he went to reward young Thomas on the superintendent's word.

He said "When I asked him jokingly what he would do with the money, he replied 'I shall buy a typewriter.' A further question brought out that he wanted to be a writer. I considered that we could do worse than to take this bright young spark and let you train him ready to take over when you retire. I felt he could do worse than to be in your capable hands, what do you think Arnold?"

"After listening to you, I think it's a doing-dong of an idea sir, a real good stroke on your part indeed. Funny how things have worked out."

Then his lordship shook hands with Thomas saying "I must be

off now, good luck young Tom. I must leave you with Arnold. He's a fine chap, he'll train you well. Listen to him Tom, and if you have any complaints at any time come and see me at once.''

Then the old gentleman left in his Rolls.

Tom and Arnold had a very long talk, with Tom finally agreeing to come and see him in three weeks time to make a start.

''Goodbye Mr Arnold'' he called. Then thrilled to the high heavens, head held high, chest squared out, young Thomas set out for home feeling like a very grown-up young man indeed. 'Fancy me,' he thought 'I could get a job as a reporter, or a columnist, or whatever they are called besides becoming a novelist on the side at first, so to speak.'

Tom marched into the kitchen, Kathy was loading up ready to leave for home.

''Hey, what happened?'' they both asked.

''Now listen to me you ladies. You do not speak to a news reporter in such tones as that.''

''Tom'' said Kathy, ''you mean you've got a job?''

''Right first time'' he replied. ''I start as a trainee reporter in three weeks' time. I've met the chap who's going to show me the ropes, and I've seen the office where I shall work, and I've met the editor, Mr Harry Black; also the report I wrote about finding the loot, will be in the paper this evening. It could be on the streets now.''

''Oh Tom, I'm so pleased for you'' said Kathy.

''I'm as happy as a big rainbow'' said Tom swinging her round and giving her a kiss.

''Tom Monkton! Really,'' said Kathy.

''Oh sorry'' replied Tom, blushing. ''I didn't mean any harm.''

His mother who was watching went into fits of laughter at her son's high spirits. Kathy joined in and soon they were all howling with laughter over this happy event that had happened to Tom.

''I'll help you with your things if you like,'' agreed Tom, ''especially if you will give me a rock cake.''

''You old fraud,'' said Kathy giving him one anyway.

They gathered up the cakes and cookies, then left for number six, watched by a very amused mother.

Tom told Kathy that there was no need to worry about paying for her mother's operation as he had over £100 in the bank. Then there would be his wages coming in.

When they arrived home Kathy took a nice hot pasty into her mum who really did enjoy it. Then she told her mother what had happened to Tom. She was full of happiness for him. She told Kathy to tell him that prayers are powerful things. Then Tom had to leave to get his tea. He told her that he would come round for an hour later.

When Tom arrived home for his tea his father was already there, and was sat at the table waiting for him, with mother telling him of Tom's luck. Eventually they all sat down to a tea of lovely fresh baked pasties with Daddie's sauce.

"Darned good tea this Mum," said Tom.

"As long as it's not Tommy's sauce you have on there young man" replied father grinning. "What's this I hear about you anyway?"

"Not a lot" said Tom. "I expect Mum told you I had a £100 reward from Lord Challenor for finding his silver."

"How nice of me to have a rich son" joked father, "now I can get a sub when I'm short."

"I shall of course consider your applications" replied Tom.

"So you've got one of those as well 'eh'!"

"Yes" replied Tom proudly, "I'm working for his lordship on his newspaper as a trainee reporter. Starting work in three weeks, then I shall take old Arnold's job as he is retiring just as soon as he's trained me."

"Your father thought you might go into the building business with him," said mother.

"I know" replied Tom, "and I would have. But Dad took Uncle Harry into a sort of partnership; then his son George left school, he went into the business. Then only last Christmas, his younger brother left school and went in — that's Dad, Uncle Harry and his two sons. If I went in I should be odd man out, so I've decided to stay out of it. No nasty thoughts meant to Dad or you, you understand."

Father was silent for a moment, then he said, "Yes Thomas." He held out his hand, Tom took it. His father said, "I'm pleased for you really. I don't see how things could have worked out if you had come in, because between you and me things aren't good. You see there is only one of me, but three of them. You could say that I felt sorry for them, which I suppose I really did. But I have the yard and the business, I have never let go of any hold on that at all. If they want it they will have to buy me out. I've told them all that I will only sell for cash. Then I would open a sort of builder's do-it-yourself shop right here in the yard and office, as sort of a one-man business."

"Dad I'm pleased to hear that you would be on your own feet, now I do feel happy about life at last. Good old Dad, and a kiss for Mum for that very nice pasty.

"Now Thomas, don't you swing me round like you did poor

Kathy mind."

"Hey" said father, "have I missed something?"

"Oh Dad, I wish you had been here" replied mother, "Tom came home so full of excitement that he picked Kathy up swung her round then kissed her. Poor Kathy was so bewildered she just shouted 'Really'. Tom just blushed and said, 'Oh sorry'. But I will say one thing, I don't mind you seeing Kathy, she is good and sensible and I like her very much."

"Me too," agreed father.

"Well mind you don't like her too much then," said Tom.

How they all laughed at his remark.

"Oh gosh" shouted Tom, "I promised Kathy I would spend an hour with her after tea. I'll go and see her and perhaps get some fish and chips. Must go" he said, getting up from the table. "Us newshounds can't be late you know."

"OK editor," replied father.

"And don't be late for bed" called mother.

"You can bet on that" replied Tom leaving amid much teasing and laughter.

CHAPTER 2

The following Monday, and with school broken up for the summer holidays, Tom decided that he would hoe through Kathy's garden and fix the clothes-line as she had asked him to do. So he set off with an old shopping bag; in it was all the tools he would require such as a hammer, pincers, staples and so on.

When he arrived at number six, his old pal Kathy seemed to be very quiet.

"What's up?" asked Tom.

"Read this," replied Kathy handing him a letter.

It was from the hospital at Brighton saying that the ambulance would collect her mother at ten o'clock on Wednesday morning to take her to the hospital for a thorough examination, and then to carry out her possible treatment.

"What's wrong with that then?" asked Tom. "It must be done, now's your chance to get it right. Your poor old mum doesn't want to stay helpless does she?"

"That's true" replied Kathy, "but Mum is in there crying now, because she says she hasn't got any money to pay the bills."

"Kathy," said Tom, "I told you once that I had £100, and out of it I would pay your mum's bill for this hospital trip, otherwise when I propose to you, you won't marry me."

"Tom Monkton, honestly," replied Kathy, "you are cheeky my lad."

"Well my dad says 'a faint heart never won a fair lady', so watch it Miss. I might even propose to you at six o'clock tonight."

"Oh Tom, you are a fool," said Kathy, "of course I will marry you, as soon as I can, but I do have to be over sixteen you know."

"I know" replied Tom, "I'm only trying to cheer you up, and I will marry you at the first opportunity. Therefore Miss, there won't be any bill, and for a start, Dad and Mum won't let you even receive one — no bill will ever come to you. So for God's sake go in

24

there and cheer your mum up, tell her Pastor Jones says there won't be any bills, that should do it. Now stop worrying while I do some work for my pretty little wife, 'nearly'.''

Kathy flushed a little red and seemed to be much happier now.

Tom set to work repairing Kathy's clothes-line and soon had it repaired ready for use. Secondly, he set to, hoed and weeded the vegetable garden. There were a few spring cabbages ready to cut, some early potatoes ready for digging, also a few young carrots. So he went off to tell Kathy.

She said, "It's no good Tom, I've got no meat to go with them."

"Listen," suggested Tom, "I'll dig some spuds, cut a nice cabbage, and pull a few carrots; now while you are getting these ready to cook, I shall pop down to the butchers and get some nice lamb chops; then when I come back I'll cut a lettuce, pull some radishes and spring onions for tea."

Tom soon brought in the veg then off to the butchers, where he bought four nice chump chops, and some beef sausages, because they had just been made; a quick dash back to Kathy, who with her apron on was preparing to cook a nice meal; while Tom got on with the gardening work.

It was a lovely day as Tom worked away, he had hung his shirt over the line working on with the warm sun on his back. Suddenly he heard someone say, "There's a good boy."

Looking up, he saw his mother going in to visit Kathy and her mum. Tom took a breather now. Then he replied "The things we menfolk do for our wives is unbelievable."

Tom's mother went into fits of laughter at her young son's dry old-fashioned way of putting things.

"Excuse me sir" she said, "it seems now that I've come to see your wife."

She went off into the kitchen to see Kathy who was very busy indeed. Kathy was so pleased to see her.

After giving her a hug she said "Auntie Gretchen, I'm so glad you've come, please read the letter. At last now we can really get our teeth into this and really make it work."

"Now Kathy, I shall be here with you, and we must get your mum's things packed into a case, then we'll follow the ambulance down to the hospital; it's about eleven miles away dear. Then we can go and visit her every week until she comes home; can I see her Kathy?"

"Yes just go in Auntie."

Mrs Monkton went in and found that Mrs Eccles had been crying.

"Hey, what's all the tears for?" asked Mrs Monkton.

"I'm not afraid to go in" replied Mrs Eccles, "it's the bills that's coming afterwards that I'm worrying about."

"There isn't going to be a bill" replied Mrs Monkton. "You won't get any bills, it's free, I wouldn't tell you a lie now would I?"

"Then there's Kathy."

"Kathy will be just fine, she will come to me, and I promise you now I shall take the greatest care of her, she'll be just fine. Now we shall give you our phone number, then if you can come out, or if you want us to know anything, your nurse can ring us from the ward office. Straight from you to us in two or three minutes, and of course we shall visit you every week and bring you anything you want. Now where's your worry?"

"Gretchen you are so sweet and kind, your husband should be proud of you, and as for young Tommy he's an absolute dear. I used to think that he and Kathy were smitten with what you might call 'puppy love', but Gretchen, I feel now, although they don't know it, they were in fact made for each other. Yes, I'm sure that they do really love each other.

"Yes I know what you mean my dear, I watch it every day. Kathy is so sensible, that I've noticed, and Tom, well he does anything he can to please her."

"Yes, you are so right my dear," agreed Mrs Eccles. They don't know it but they are deeply in love. We must guide and help them in their tender years, because one thing we can't do is part them, that would be impossible now, neither would stand for that and the unhappiness would break their young hearts."

'Yes' agreed both women, 'all we can do is guide them.' They would do their best for their children's deep love.

Kathy came in then with tea for the two mums.

"I expect Tom could do with one," said Mrs Eccles.

"No, he's in the kitchen and he's already had two," replied Kathy "and he's hoping for a third. He's eating sandwiches of lettuce, spring onions, and radishes."

"That lad is always hungry" said Tom's mother.

"Yes," agreed Kathy, "he's just told me how hungry news-men get."

The women howled with laughter. "It's only so that you will make endless piles of sandwiches for him" warned Auntie Gretchen.

"I know" replied Kathy who was still crying with laughter, "but I never had the heart to disillusion him."

They all had a good laugh at scheming Thomas.

"Well I do feel so much better now," said Mrs Eccles.

"And so you should" replied Kathy, "you've been in the dumps too long Mum."

"I've brought a basket of goodies for you today Kathy."

"Thank you very much Auntie, and do you know Tom has dug some early potatoes, and cut a nice cabbage? He also pulled young carrots, and he grew them all Auntie."

"Yes but all the same, he does tease you know."

"Yes" agreed Kathy. "I know alright, but sometimes he is very serious and really means what he says, I know that too. Anyway he went off to the butchers and came back with some lovely lamb chump chops, so I was able to make a nice cooked meal. He even picked some some mint up by the currant bushes to cook with the potatoes. I must go now" said Kathy, "to see to this hungry newsman." Off she went giggling.

"Can you see what I mean now my dear?" said Gretchen.

"Yes I saw what you meant alright, really it's sweet to watch."

While the two women made plans about going into hospital, Kathy finished cooking the lunch, and Thomas continued to work until he had done the whole garden, including the front flower beds.

"I'll see you after tea" called Mrs Monkton as she left to get her husband's midday meal.

"See you later," shouted Tom as he packed up his tools putting them away in the shed. All the rubbish, weeds and bits he put on the compost heap, then grabbing his shirt from the line he shouted, "After tea then. I must earn some wages at the golf course this afternoon then I'll bring fish and chips after tea."

"You can stop here for your lunch Tom," shouted Kathy.

"Mum's expecting me home" replied Tom. "Well I suppose she is anyway."

"There and I've cooked plenty for you" said Kathy.

"There you go again" replied Tom, "twisting my arm by making it smell good. Well only a small lot then," he replied.

Kathy dished him up a meal. After taking in her mother's on a tray they both sat down to enjoy the meal that Kathy had cooked.

As they ate it Tom said, "You leave school at Christmas. What shall you do if your mum is OK?"

"Well I must get a job to help out."

"Yeah sure, a good idea" agreed Tom.

"But we've got to get this hospital job behind us first" said Kathy. "I'm going down to your mum this afternoon to borrow a suitcase for mum to take her things into hospital with, because hers is too big, and I've got to have a look at your spare room."

"Nice room that," said Tom. "You go up four more steps from the top of the stairs and there you have the spare room together with its own bathroom. Like a small flat it is, you see there are two bathrooms in the house, so you will have it just fine at your end.''

After the meal Tom said "Must go to work now." He stood up to go, then said "Let me explain before I leave. Never ever," he continued walking up to Kathy, "go off to work without kissing your wife goodbye."

Then he gave her a kiss and ran quickly from the room, leaving poor Kathy taken completely by surprise.

All she could do was to shout, "Hey!"

"Bye for now" called Tom, as he left on his bike and sped off like the wind.

When he came home for his tea, his mother said "Now look Tom I will tell you the arrangements that we have made for tomorrow. Dad will get his car out and take Kathy and me down to the hospital following behind the ambulance — you may come if you wish."

"What time will you be coming home then?" asked Tom.

"About twelve I should think, perhaps a bit later."

"Well I'll stay home and make sure the kettle is on."

"As you wish" replied mother. "I'll go and see Kathy for an hour after tea then, I'll see her when she comes back" agreed Tom thoughtfully.

"I bet she'll be very pleased when it's all over" said mother. "I've got her room ready and she likes it very much."

"Good," replied Tom, "after all it's like a small flat up there really."

"Yes," agreed mother "and with God on our side perhaps she won't need it for long."

That evening Tom sat and talked to Kathy. Mainly he talked of what they could do when her mother came back from hospital. This he thought would give her hope and it did really seem to work. When he left Kathy he said, "Don't forget the specialist said it could take up to twelve weeks, that means that when she gets back we must feed her up. We can grow lots of veg, and I could catch fish from the pier — it will all help. Well I'll see you tomorrow old pal." Then he gave her cheek a quick kiss and left for home.

In the morning Tom got up early, off he went to the beach to test his fishing rod which he hadn't used for some time. He dug up some worms and finally caught two flat-fish from off the pier. He went off home now quite happily to breakfast, showing his catch to his mother who agreed they could make someone a nice meal.

His father fetched his car ready for the off, then his parents went to see if they could help Kathy or her mother.

As they pulled up in front of number six an ambulance pulled up behind them. The driver asked for the front door to be opened, and in a jiffy they seemed to have Mrs Eccles on to the stretcher and were bringing her out. They put her straight up into the ambulance. "One can ride with her" they said.

Without hesitation Mrs Monkton climbed in. Kathy carrying her mother's suitcase got into the car with Mr Monkton. "I have locked up" she said. Off they went behind the ambulance heading for the hospital.

The ambulance seemed to really speed along at times — it was hard to keep it in sight. Kathy was being very brave.

"I'm glad you are so sensible about this" said Mr Monkton to her.

"Well," she replied, "it's Tom really. "We talked last night of all the things we can do and the places we can go when mother is well again and can look after herself."

"Yes of course, and when Tom is old enough to drive he'll soon have a car of his own. You can bet your boots on that" said Mr Monkton. "Now I'll tell you a secret, even now he can drive quite well."

As they neared the hospital Mr Monkton let the ambulance get ahead. He made out that he couldn't pass another car on purpose. By the time they arrived the ambulance was already empty and Kathy's mother was in the ward.

"We must wait a minute while they put her in bed. Auntie will be out to tell us when we can go in."

He just didn't want little Kathy to see her mother being carried into the hospital and had succeeded.

After a while Gretchen came out onto the steps, looking around the car park; seeing them she signalled and Kathy came running with the suitcase.

"Everything is just fine" said Auntie. "She's in bed right in the corner on the left as you go in the door. She seems to like it."

They went in and gave her mother the case. Mother seemed quite happy and settled already. After chatting for a few minutes, two nurses came and they had to leave. They had promised to visit on Sunday afternoon, Kathy felt a bit sad now, a lump in the throat feeling. Mr Monkton drove out of town to a small tea-house, where they sat down to tea; bread and butter, and cakes.

"I wonder what Master Thomas is up to?" said Mrs Monkton. "I feel that he's got something up his sleeve. Anyway with your mum settled now, let's go and find out."

Off they went with Kathy obviously feeling much better.

Mr Monkton gave his wife a sly wink as they travelled along. They were all in a much better mood now. At last they pulled into the yard — the clock in the car dashboard showed it was ten-past twelve. As they came up to the back door, they saw a figure in a white apron dashing about singing 'Tiptoe through the Tulips'.

Father opened the door quietly motioning the others to be quiet as they all crept inside and stood still. Suddenly Thomas turned to go back to the table which he had neatly laid out for lunch, when he saw them all standing there.

"My God, burglars," he shouted clutching the right hand side of his chest.

Everyone burst out laughing. Kathy ran to him, threw her arms around him telling him how cute he was. Tom took his chance to wink at his parents — they both winked back. Soon everyone forgot their troubles. Tom told them how he was planning a big surprise, he told them how far he had got cooking the meal. First he said, I cheated a bit (as usual), they all chorused laughing at him. He told them how he went out and bought some cooked beef; he had it sliced and had cooked it again in the frying pan in gravy. Then he had peeled potatoes, shelled peas, and had cooked them and some carrots.

"Now it's just about ready" he said. "I reckon that I deserve some thanks after slaving away over a hot stove; and the afters are in the oven warming up."

Kathy in her haste to help undid his apron and put it on herself. Mrs Monkton joined in the work and soon had a meal fashioned out of what Tom had done. When they looked in the oven they howled with laughter.

"You big cheat" they said.

Tom had bought some ready-to-eat apple pies and was warming them up. He had also bought two cartons of fresh dairy cream to go with them.

At last they sat down to the meal and funnily enough it tasted quite nice, even to the apple pie and cream. How they all pulled the cook's leg over this, 'never to be forgotten meal'.

As they sat now enjoying a cup of tea, Auntie Gretchen told Kathy how Master Thomas once made a stew. She explained how Tom's father and herself went out to go to a sale.

"It could take a long time" she explained to Tom, so he didn't want to go.

"It could be very dreary" he told them.

While they were at the sale Tom decided that he dare not try to cook a meal, but he thought he could make a stew. So he went next door to Mrs Harris and told her of his plan. Now she made some pastry for him as he had asked her. Off he went now to get some meat.

"I need beef for a stew" he told the butcher.

The butcher was tickled pink for such a little chap to be making a stew, so he chopped it up for him, wrapped up some suet, and told him it was for the dumplings.

Thomas decided on a big saucepan because he was so hungry. In it he put the dumplings, into which he had pressed lumps of suet. He chopped up three large onions, all the beef, two large potatoes, then he set it on the gas to boil. It had boiled for about an hour when Mrs Harris looked in. She came in looked at the stew and told him he needed to make it thicker.

"Squash up a Syminton's soup square" she suggested "and stir it in."

But this did not do the trick. Then he hit on a great idea, so he stirred in three handfuls of Quaker oats.

After about twenty minutes we came home, there he was standing on a chair stirring it because he was too small to reach. His soup was so thick by now that he could scarcely move the spoon. Oh how we laughed — but it wasn't until we had eaten it that he told us what was in it. But believe me it tasted very nice. How little Kathy laughed, she pictured Tom quite small with a determined look on his face making a stew for his mum. Yes agreed Auntie, he was so serious about the whole thing, even the dumplings into which he had pushed lumps of suet tasted quite reasonable.

"Well you just got to acquire the right technique for this cooking lark you see Dad, like cheating a bit."

"You'll make a good cook yet" he said.

There was lots of laughing while mother and Kathy did the washing-up.

Father went off to work, while mother, Kathy and Tom went round to number six to collect Kathy's things and to tidy up. While the two ladies were tidying up, Tom carried a case round to the room that Kathy was going to use, then he was to go straight back to see if anything else was needed to be carried. As he was coming down the stairs, the phone started to ring. Tom answered it, the caller was the hospital matron asking for Kathy.

"She's not here at the moment, but I can take a message," said Tom.

He took the message and ran all the way back to Kathy.

"Why are you running like that for, silly?" she asked.

"Phone call," replied Tom, trying to get his breath back. "Hospital" he puffed.

"Is everything alright?" asked mother.

"Yes," he puffed getting control a bit. "I was just leaving when the phone rang. The matron was on the line, puff, puff! She said that Mrs Eccles had had her examination in the operating theatre, and that they had already started her treatment, she was quite comfortable, and we could ring tomorrow evening just before seven. Good news 'eh?" asked Tom.

"Very good news indeed," replied mother.

Kathy started to smile a bit now, and soon they were all chatting away happily.

"I think we ought to scrub up and do some painting while she's having her treatment, don't you?" suggested mother.

"It's a good chance to do it" agreed Tom.

"But I can't afford the paint and paper," said Kathy.

"Your troubles are solved" replied Tom.

"How's that?" asked Kathy.

"Because me dear, there is a rich newshound in your midst, he will buy all that is needed."

They laughed at Tom.

"Bless my soul" replied mother, "your father will have all we need in the yard, I expect."

"I'm well aware of that" agreed Tom.

"Oh you fraud, accused the ladies."

It was all settled what they would do, and Tom had volunteered to do the work.

When they had finished their tidying up they went back to the yard. Kathy and Mrs Monkton went to the bedroom to get everything ready for Kathy's first night away from home. Tom went to the yard office to see what his father had in paint and wallpaper. He found quite a few rolls of wallpaper which he put on one side; as for paint there seemed to be lots. "I'll ask Father about this when he comes home, maybe I can get it for nothing," he said to himself with a chuckle.

Father came home to find the ladies listening to Tom. They seemed to be highly amused as he told them about the very hard life he led now that he was a rich news reporter, almost.

Father peeped in, listened for awhile, then he said "I feel like I've missed something old son."

"You certainly have Dad, if I could remember what I've just said I would even repeat the same lies for you."

Father and mother both knew that Tom was only larking about, trying to take little Kathy's mind from worrying too much about her mother. Therefore, of course, they joined in his nonsense.

As they ate their tea mother broached the subject of redecorating Kathy's home. It seemed such a good opportunity now that her mother was away for awhile.

"Splendid idea" agreed father, "something for you both to do and a nice surprise for Kathy's mother as well. There are plenty of materials in the sheds, just help yourselves, and while I think of it why don't you two get yourselves off to the flicks tonight, then tomorrow you can pick out the colours you want and get cracking on this redecorating job."

"What do you think Kathy?" asked Tom.

"Oh yes please" she said, "I haven't been to the pictures for ages."

"There's your answer news-man, off you go."

"Oh yes," said Kathy, "I must tell you Uncle Frank. I've had a phone call from the hospital. They said that Mum's had her examination and they have started her treatment."

"Really, well now," replied Uncle Frank, "this seems like they know what's wrong."

"You think it's good news then?" asked Kathy.

"Yes, I'd say it's got to be; you see normally they don't ring you; but I expect your mother asked them to. Now let's go over it again, they said that your mother has had her examination, and they have now started her treatment. That means that they must know what is wrong, otherwise how could they have started her treatment. It simply means they have started to put it right. 'Great news indeed', the best I've heard all day."

Kathy was thrilled to bits with this explanation, "Yippee" she shouted. "Come on Thomas, we're off out on the town to celebrate the good news."

"OK baby, let's hit the trail," agreed Thomas rushing off to get ready.

It wasn't long before they left the house heading for the High Street, leaving it quiet and peaceful for Mr and Mrs Monkton. She looked at her husband who was smiling to himself.

"What do you make of those two father?"

"They are lovely to watch," he replied. "Young Kathy thinks the world of Tom you know, and as for Tom, well he's just devoted to her. You see my dear, if they grow up like they are at this moment in time, by the time they are say, twenty-one, they must surely be a perfect match for life."

"Yes, I know exactly what you are trying to say, I feel the same, and so does Kathy's mother, and by the way what do you think of things so far?"

"Well I like what I hear" replied father. "We can only take our cue from the Lord — just watch and pray — I feel that everything will be OK eventually."

c

A knock on the door came at that point.

"I'll go" said Mrs Monkton. "I'm nearest."

Back she came with Pastor Jones.

"Oh I'm sorry," he apologized. "I thought you may well have finished your tea."

"We've finished alright" replied Mrs Monkton, "only we've just got the two young ones off to the pictures. You see we've got Kathy staying here from tonight while her mother is away."

"Good idea to send them to the pictures" agreed Pastor Jones.

"You see" said Mrs Monkton, "we had to endure a long talk from Thomas about the very hard life he leads now that he is a hardworking news reporter, nearly. He does these funny talks to try and keep Kathy happy."

"Yes, bless him," replied Pastor Jones. "You know I'm as pleased as punch with young Thomas, finding that loot as he calls it, then landing that job. He's a caution and no mistake; but I expect you are sorry Frank that he didn't join you in the business?"

"No not really, if he wants to find his own feet, then I'll help him."

"You can't force him to go into a job he doesn't like."

"He'll settle one day" suggested Mrs Monkton, "but I must admit he really can write."

"There is another point I like about him" said Pastor Jones, "he really does look after that little lady when she's with him."

"Yes, we were just saying" agreed Mr Monkton, "just before you came in about how much we have observed that they like each other. Young Kathy's mother has noticed as well."

"Ah! now that brings me to why I've visited you this evening," replied the Pastor. "I must tell you before I forget it. Now I've just had a long talk on the phone with Doctor Harrington."

"Oh dear," exclaimed Mrs Monkton.

"Fear not," replied Pastor Jones, "just listen to this. Now it seems that Doctor Harrington had Mrs Eccles down to the operating theatre to carry out his final examinations. He discovered that his first diagnosis was correct. She had a large internal cyst, which was pressing on some nerves pinching them and causing her great pain; and also it was causing her to lose the use of her legs. Now he has operated and has successfully removed the cyst, which I'm thankful to say was not malignant. But however, it was quite large causing her great pain, as you well know of course. Already she is out of pain and has started to feel the use of her legs. Doctor Harrington says she will be in hospital now for about three weeks, then she can come home. She can have visitors of course, and will need her clothes very soon. He says as soon as the operation has healed up sufficiently, he will get her out of bed, a little each day at first of course, until she can walk properly again. You can take in plenty of fruit for her to eat and he thinks the cure will be 100 per cent; say in two months from now."

Mrs Monkton was now overwhelmed with great happiness, tears of joy ran down her cheeks. She said "Thank you Lord for hearing our prayers."

"Where would we be without him?" replied her husband. Whereupon all three of them knelt and thanked God from the depth of their souls.

"What a happy little girl is going to bed in this house tonight," said Pastor Jones.

"Yes she leaves school at Christmas, so that will be a big celebration for her with the news-man of course," said father.

"Of course" agreed Pastor Jones smiling, "they even come to church hand-in-hand — it's so sweet to see them."

"Yes" agreed Mrs Monkton, "we've all decided to help and guide them; that of course includes Kathy's mother, because by observing them as we do, we realize that it goes much deeper than puppy love, to coin a phrase. We all realize that it's a very deep natural God-given love. They don't even realize it yet, you see they are not aware of it, therefore we think they need clever guidance."

"How very wise," agreed Pastor Jones. "What a good line to take indeed. Kathy will come to no harm when she is with young Thomas, that's for sure. May God bless them both and keep them safe."

Pastor Jones had to leave then as he had more visits to make.

Mrs Monkton tidied up the room, then sat by the fire with her husband who was now sound asleep. After a while the peace of the house was shattered by the returning youngsters.

"We've brought 'chish and fips' Mum," announces Tom. "They are quite hot."

"Did you enjoy the film dear?" asked Mrs Monkton.

"Yes it was lovely" replied Kathy. "We liked it very much."

As they all sat down to supper, father said "Tell Kathy about Pastor Jones's visit."

"Tell me as well" replied Tom. "He's my 'bestest' pal."

So mother told them that Pastor Jones came, just after they went out and he had said he had been talking to Doctor Harrington on the phone and he told him that Kathy's mum has had her operation. It was only a very large cyst which had been pressing on some nerves, causing her to lose the use of her legs. Already she can feel and use her toes, and move her legs quite a bit without pain;

she must stay in bed for awhile, to let the operation heal. But on Sunday we must take her in some clothes to wear, because soon she will be out of bed for a while each day to make her stronger, then in about three weeks' time, she can come home. The doctor also says that she should be completely cured eventually.

Kathy cried tears of joy. Tom lent her his handkerchief while she cried and laughed with happiness. She was really happy now.

"We must really pull our fingers out and get on with that painting," suggested Tom. "Three weeks will soon pass."

"Do you know" said Kathy, "I really thought I would lose my mum, just like I did my dad."

"Yes we did know how you felt," replied Mrs Monkton, "don't worry anymore now dear, just pray and be thankful."

So Kathy said "I don't really know how I could have coped without you all. Auntie Gretchen how can I ever thank you?"

"Don't ever think about it. You see dear, God put us here to help you bear your troubles. All you have to do is to just thank God for his great loving mercy for answering your prayers.

Later that evening a happy group of people went to bed in that house, I can tell you!

Auntie Kitt causes trouble.
Tom gets his calling.

CHAPTER 3

The next day, Tom and Kathy were busy stripping the walls of the sitting-room at number six, when who should call on Mrs Monkton — none other than Auntie Kitt; whose husband and sons worked with Mr Monkton.

"Hello! it's not often we see you around here," said Mrs Monkton.

"No it isn't" replied Auntie Kitt, "I'm here on an errand for my husband·and two sons, and I sincerely hope that you will see sense and agree to my proposals."

"And what are they may I ask?" said Mrs Monkton.

"It's simply this; that you and your husband move out of this house into mine, and we will move in here. We will pay you five pounds per week until we have paid for the business. I have three men in my house — you haven't. I have three men in the business, you only have one, therefore, out of fairness you should do as I say."

"Well now" replied Gretchen, "here's my answer. Firstly, it's up to my husband, it's his business. Grandad left it to him, and it wouldn't matter if you had twenty sons in the business, you won't get it, and what's more we shall never move out of here, therefore I suggest you ask my husband, I am only his wife who must honour and obey. When Grandad was ill, no one would look after him, and that includes you. We did it out of our Christian decency; then when he died he left us the business, together with the house and yard; so you see madam, it's all in my husband's hands."

"I expected an answer like that," snapped Auntie Kitt. "That no good son of yours must have been mixed up with that robbery, otherwise how did he know where to find the stolen goods? Answer me that," she shouted.

"That's easy" replied Gretchen. She spun Auntie Kitt round and pushed her from the room, slamming the door shut behind her.

Gretchen heard her through the door, shouting, "You'll hear more about this, you'll wish you did as I suggested." Then she stormed off muttering to herself.

'Well my girl' thought Gretchen, 'it looks like the battle is on at last. We have been expecting it, I must admit. I wonder what she'll do next.' Then she shrugged it off, put some things in a bag and went off to see Tom and Kathy.

When she arrived at number six, there they were busy as two bees, scraping and damping down the walls. Kathy was busy sweeping up the mess.

"Oh my, we are busy" said auntie, as she walked in.

"Don't stop us" called Tom.

"I'll do as you say" replied mother. "Now Kathy, I'm afraid dear you will have to eat all these cakes."

"Coming mother" called Tom.

"My oh my, we do change our minds quickly" said mother, winking at Kathy.

"Well you see it's like this" replied Tom, "us painters and decorators really do get hungry. It's the smell from the paint you know. Did you know mother" continued Tom, "that if you don't eat . . . what did you bring?"

"Cakes" replied mother.

"That's it, see how clever you are, like I was saying if you don't eat cakes when you are a painter and decorator you can easily get painter's colic."

"Oh you fraud," said mother, "you aren't even using paint."

"I'll darn soon alter that" he replied. "I'll open the first pot now."

"You are a crafty old thing" said mother as she called "Come and get it."

"The other other day Kathy, it was us newshounds. Today is quite different" replied Tom, "we are first-class painters, and Kathy is my painter's mate."

How the ladies laughed at Tom.

They had their break and went quickly back to work. Mother stayed for a while enjoying the company of the youngsters. 'They are so resilient' she thought. 'Trouble runs off their backs like water. Just look at them thoroughly enjoying the work and each other's company.'

"Lunch at one you two," said mother as she left, with Kathy shouting, "We'll be there Auntie."

Mr Monkton came home to his lunch and heard all that had happened with Auntie Kitt.

"You treated her very politely" said father. They were both still laughing when the two youngsters came home for their lunch.

"How's life with you two?" asked Mr Monkton.

"We have done one wall in the sitting-room" replied Tom, "we could finish it today, then we'll be painting tomorrow."

"I hope you have cleaned the walls first?"

"Yes" replied Tom "and sized them."

"Good man" agreed father, "and I hope you are pasting the paper and not the wall."

"How did you guess?" smiled Tom.

"So" announced father, "my training was not in vain then. You see mother, if the worst comes to the worst, as they say, he could take over from me."

"Dead easy" replied Tom, winking at Kathy.

Eventually Mr Monkton went back to work saying to his wife, "We shall see what we shall see my dear."

Kathy wanted to help with the washing-up.

"I can manage just fine my dear, now off you go you have so much to do."

By the time they had to leave for tea, all the papering was done.

"It should be dry by morning, then we'll put the frieze up and start painting. By the weekend this room will be ready, then it's the kitchen, that will want the walls washed down with Sugar Soap," said Tom.

"Whatever is Sugar Soap?" asked Kathy.

"Well it's stuff you put in a bucket of hot water, then you can clean down the walls with it."

"Tom Monkton you are pulling my leg again" replied Kathy.

"Good Lord girl, I thought everybody knew what Sugar Soap was.

Kathy laughed and said "You don't kid me this time."

Off home they went with Kathy thinking that she had caught Tom out this time, because he kept quiet about this Sugar Soap.

When they arrived home for tea, Kathy was still laughing.

"What's he been saying now?" asked auntie.

"Well he says he's going to wash the walls in the kitchen with Sugar Soap."

"Yes that's the correct thing to use, dear." Tom came into the room now with a cardboard box about $8'' \times 4'' \times 2''$, with the words 'Sugar Soap' on it. He gave it to Kathy without a word. Off he went now to take off his overalls and wash his hands. "Yes, that's the stuff" confirmed mother as Tom came back.

Kathy said "Sorry Tom for disbelieving you."

"That's alright" replied Tom, "I always tell the truth." Then he could contain himself no longer. He laughed at Kathy and gave her a kiss saying, "Sorry I teased you."

Mother came then with two fresh boiled eggs, each with some lovely bread and butter, and a dish of fancy cakes to finish off with.

"We're going for a nice walk along the beach tonight Mum," announced Tom.

After tea they got themselves ready and set off intending to go to the beach. But, as they passed the bus depot, Tom noticed a bus that was standing there. It was going to Pulborough via Stonedene.

"Tell you what," said Tom, "let's get some fish and chips, jump on that bus and go over to Stonedene. It's only three miles away, we could visit my great aunt and uncle — they don't get many visitors you see — and I haven't seen them for ages. Mum and Dad go over, but I usually stay at home to write or something."

"Well if you really think we should," replied Kathy.

"Look we got just ten minutes. You wait here by the bus while I run next door to the chippies. Now if I miss it it's just too bad.

Then Tom hurried into the chip shop. No one in yet, so he bought four suppers with extra chips, then he raced back to Kathy with his carrier bag of goodies.

"Can we get on board sir?" asked Tom of a chap standing near, wearing a driver's cap.

"Sure" he replied, "we shall leave in about two minutes."

Three men and a woman got on then. The bus, a single decker, set off over the downs. It stopped outside a pub called the Plough. It was right in the middle of the tiny village of Stonedene.

"Thank you" called Tom, as they got off.

They walked along to a farm just a stone's throw away, a sign on the gate was 'Bournend Farm'.

"In here" said Tom.

As they went up to the back door, Kathy noticed an elderly lady using a separator. On seeing Tom coming she stopped working, and said "Bless my soul! If it isn't Master Thomas."

"Hello Auntie Liz," replied Tom, "how are you?"

"Oh not too bad Tom; my old knee plays me up a bit, otherwise I'm fine."

"Poor old Auntie" said Tom.

"Now who's this nice little gal, you've got with you then?"

"Oh sorry, this is my 'bestest' pal — this is Kathy."

"How do you do," said auntie shaking hands with her. "Have you known Thomas very long?" she asked.

"Oh yes," replied Kathy, "for quite a few years."

"Even longer," said Tom. "Where's Uncle Joe?" he enquired.

"Sleeping in his chair in the kitchen," replied auntie. "Joe, Joe," she shouted.

"Ello" answered Uncle Joe. "What's up?"

"Visitors," replied Aunt Liz.

"Visitors!" answered uncle coming into the kitchen doorway clutching his walking stick. "Well, well," said Joe, "it's our Tom. How's tricks then?"

"Great, Uncle Joe," replied Tom "and please Uncle Joe will you meet my buddie, Kathy."

Uncle Joe shook hands with Kathy and welcomed her to the farm.

"She's a nice little gal Tom," teased uncle. "Now come on in both of you."

"I've got a fish and chip supper here in the bag," said Tom. "It's still quite hot and it's freshly cooked — I asked the man when I got them."

"Well, I suppose you came over on the bus then?"

"Yes, I thought you might like a fish and chip supper."

Aunt Liz took the bag saying, "I'll get them ready."

"Oh please can I help you?" asked Kathy.

"Yes if you like my dear."

Kathy dashed off to help poor old hobbling Aunt Liz.

"Yes, that's the plates my dear; knives and forks over there; and the table-cloth is lying on the dresser. In the cupboard is bread, butter, vinegar, salt, pepper and so on."

Auntie Liz was most amazed to see a young lady dashing about laying the table for her. Then Kathy carried in the plates of food. Uncle Joe was talking to Tom, saying how very hard he finds it to run the farm now that his leg had gone stiff.

As they all sat eating their supper, the youngsters told aunt and uncle all about Kathy's troubles, and how things had started to work well for her at last.

They all had a nice talk, then Uncle Joe said, "While you makes a pot of tea Lizzie, I'll just pop along to see if my old sow is alright."

"Can I come?" asked Tom.

"Sure you can old son, and welcome."

"Then can I help Auntie Liz?" asked Kathy.

"Yes if you like my dear" came auntie's reply.

"I'll wash up for you then" she said, and she quickly had the plates collected before old auntie could turn round.

Now Uncle Joe and Tom toddled off up the yard to the pigsties.

"This old sow is due to farrow anytime now, I have to keep my eye on her because she has a habit of laying on her young 'uns'."

Tom noticed that old Uncle Joe had a lot of trouble getting into the sty. He waited outside.

"Good Lord," Tom heard him say. "She's got two already! No three! So far so good. We'll leave her now and I'll look in later."

After a struggle, old uncle managed to get out of the sty. He stood for a moment to get his leg right.

"Trouble is Tom," he said, "since my accident, I find it very hard to get about, and of course you can't get help for love nor money. You see all the youngsters flock into the town; they got to get a pansy's job indoors; the younger generation just ain't tough enough anymore. My God boy, when young men won't tackle a proper man's job, it's a darn sad day for old England that's what."

At that point a piglet squealed.

"Darn that blooming sow, she's laid on one."

Tom never waited one second, he leapt over the gate, bent down and went into the sty's doorway and was able to rescue the piglet which ran off grunting its thanks. Tom counted — out he went saying "She's got seven now Uncle Joe. What help do you want here then?" he asked his great uncle.

"Well, a good intelligent chap, would do fine. One who could handle the tractor and be taught farming from A to Z. But it's a real tough man's job," he explained. "He must be able to stand all weathers and be a good farmer."

As they toddled back towards the house. Tom was silent for awhile. Then he stopped dead in his tracks, with his feet apart and his hand thrust deep into his trouser pockets, chin out, he said, "Right Uncle Joe, can you give me some advice?"

"Sure if I can," replied his uncle who was looking at him in an amused sort of way.

"Well," said Tom, "now if a man says he's going to do something, he's got to do it."

"Sure enough," replied Joe.

"Well, I promised Kathy that I would redecorate some rooms for her, it will take most of next week. The other thing is if a man says he will start work on a job, then changes his mind, can he resign and not even start work?"

"Sure," replied Uncle Joe, "just send a letter of explanation."

A smile spread slowly over young Tom's face, "That's the answer then. Uncle Joe, you just got yourself a darned good farmer. Yes, sir, you do talk a lot of common sense. Yes sir, I'm your man."

Another squeal sent Tom racing across the yard. He leapt the gate, ran into the pig house, and was able to rescue yet another piglet. Out he came.

"Uncle Joe" he shouted, "you are now the proud father of nine."

Uncle Joe could stand it no longer, he just stood there and howled with laughter at young Tom.

"Oh dear, oh dear, Thomas, I've been keeping my eye on you and you are a Monkton through and through." He held out his hand saying, "Now if you are sure, then welcome aboard, Thomas, I'd just love a young Monkton here with me."

Tom shook hands with his great uncle then he said "You'll be able to take it easy, just as soon as I can get here. You just say the job, I'll soon do it or burst" he added.

They went indoors. Tom washed his hands and they all sat down to a nice pot of tea.

"Now Thomas," said auntie, "I just want to say this to you. Mind you take great care of this little gal here; she's a real treasure and no mistake."

"Oh yes, I always look after Kathy, she's my pal. My buddie, and my gal. Sometimes I call her my old ball and chain. You like her then?"

"Yes I do" replied auntie, "very much."

By now Uncle Joe was just howling with laughter, "I've never heard of anybody being called a ball and chain before," he said.

"Well now, Auntie, I must tell you I'm going to help Uncle Joe here on the farm."

"Honest Tom?" inquired Kathy.

"It sure is honest, ask Uncle Joe," replied Tom. "You see Kathy, to be a farmer you just have got to have it, if you haven't got it, then you are no good. Now folks," said Tom, sticking his chin out, "I've got it. Now you see Kathy, us farmers just gotta be tough, like Uncle Joe and me. For instance you could be out on the downs minding your sheep, there you are just about to bring them down for tea — suddenly a violent thunderstorm breaks, sheets of heavy rain, big blue flashes of lightning striking down, darn great peals of thunder — all your sheep panic and scatter in all directions." Tom was waving his arms about, then he said, "You've just gotta move, like you never moved before. Now to round them all up, you go haring about like a bat out of hell; all over the downs."

Dear old Uncle Joe could stand it no longer, he just plain howled, holding his sides with great peals of laughter until the tears rolled down his cheeks. Auntie Liz, was no better off, it took a few minutes to calm them down.

Then Uncle Joe, when he was able to speak said, "What with his ball and chain, and then going like a bat out of hell, he's going to be some busy, I can see."

"Have you got any horses?" asked Tom.

"No cart-horses, only a cob. Now I'll tell you what I do — I puts the horse in the old milk float, then I ties the harrows on the back, then I sits up in the float, and away we go, harrowing. Got to get about somehow, you see Tom. We've only got two cows now, had to get rid of 'em — I just can't cope you see."

"Fear not, Uncle Joe, it's Tom Monkton to the rescue."

"Good for you Tom. I do hope so. Oh by the way" said auntie, "how are you getting home tonight? Only you got twenty minutes to catch the bus outside the Plough."

"Right" replied Kathy, collecting up the cups and things, "I'll wash up for you."

Auntie went hobbling off to fill a shopping bag with things for mother. Soon they were ready to leave, after promising to see them soon. They left hand-in-hand, Tom carrying the bag.

"We'll bike over next time," he suggested "then we can see how long it takes. Do you know Uncle Joe had nine piglets born while we were there tonight? When they are weaned they could be worth £3-10-0 each. That would be about £30 profit. Now if I had ten sows, that's £300. Yeah, I reckon a lot to this farming lark."

The bus arrived, the driver took a parcel into the pub then off went the bus for home. They hurried along with Kathy holding tight to Tom's arm in order to keep up with him. Like Tom told her, farmers must walk fast because they got so much work to do. Straight indoors they marched, to find mum and dad dozing in the chairs.

"Hello" said mother, "haven't I seen that bag before."

"Yeah, Aunt Liz sent it over for you."

Tom gave her the bag. She took out two pots of honey, some jars of pickles, a dozen eggs, and about two pounds of fresh butter. There was a small note which said, *Hope you find this useful.*

"How is Aunt Liz?" enquired mother.

"Oh same as usual."

"And Uncle Joe?"

"He's OK, but says his leg has gone completely stiff now. We were going for a walk along the beach, but we saw the bus waiting for Stonedene, and there was no queue so we took a fish and chip supper over to them. We never did go for a walk."

"His honey is always good," said father as he looked at a pot of old honey.

"You mean Uncle Joe keeps bees?" asked Tom.

"Yes he's got about ten swarms down at the far end of the orchard. That's how he always grows such nice apples, plenty of pollinators around you see."

"Dad, can I ask you a question?" said Tom. "It's very important to me, and I'm honestly not larking about. This is serious, real serious."

"OK son, then let's sort it out 'eh."

Kathy and mother were in the kitchen making a pot of tea — leaving them together.

"Look" said Tom, "I don't know where to start really, but something made me go over to Bournend Farm tonight. I don't know what it was, but something seemed to just guide me. I didn't say anything to Kathy, we just went. When we got there I was still aware that something was pulling me, I can't explain that any better. Auntie Liz immediately took to Kathy. She just adores her — told me I had better look after her, or else. If she only knew how I feel about Kathy, she would never have said that, but of course I understand. But Uncle Joe, now that's different; Dad I felt awful, poor old Uncle Joe, there he is still trying to struggle on with his leg, which will never ever get any better. God only knows how he does it. As I looked at him I realized that he was a true Monkton and no mistake. You see Dad, he's really facing great odds, what with his age and all. That's when I got this awful feeling in my chest, a sickly feeling, as though I had been caught out and was now being accused. You know it's the first time I've ever felt tears in my eyes. I said 'Can't you get help Uncle Joe?' He said 'He had a man, old Tom Marshall, but he couldn't work anymore, he'd got a bad heart you see.' He had tried and tried, but couldn't get anybody, seems like fate was against him, he said 'All the so-called young men seem to go for a cissy job, in a shop or office. Yes Tom,' he said, 'it's a sad day for dear old England when young men turn out to be cissies instead of good down to earth God-fearing farmers.' That's when something snapped in me. Dad, Mum, I never wanted to go to work in that office. I said 'yes', because it's not fair for me to scrounge on you always. You brought me up, that's understandable, and fair. Now I want to work and fight my own way. Mum, Dad, I just got to help Uncle Joe, he's a wonderful old man, and God knows he deserves help. Yet despite all his troubles he can still laugh."

"OK son, I do understand, go to it eh. To tell you the truth Tom, both your mother and me never thought the paper a good job for you. You are a bit of a tough egg. Look Tom, how could you report on a meeting of the Church Ladies' Guild, or some pansy council meeting, or write about a new shop opening. Oh yes, you could do it but for how long can my son stay a cissy. Your own words Tom, now old son I can help you."

Kathy was laying the table now for a pot of tea and some beef sandwiches. As they ate together, father then explained to Tom that his great grandfather who's name was also Thomas Monkton, came up from Wiltshire many years ago and bought Bournend Farm; he was a good farmer. "Then my father, that's your grandfather, came here and started this business. Because you see the farm in those days could not support many people. Now your grandfather's brother, that's your great Uncle Joe, he stayed at home and helped his father. That's how things have got like they are today. As you can see great Uncle Joe never had any children, that shows you what he's up against. That's why I said go to it son. I reckon you have had your guidance given to you tonight. If you feel like writing later on, you should certainly gain some good experiences to write about. After all, farmers really do need some good writers to explain their problems and no mistake. Now mother, in order to help him, will you please order the *Farmer's Weekly*"? asked father.

"Yes first thing tomorrow," mother answered.

"Now Kathy, can you see him in his farmer's uniform?" said father with a wink.

"Uniform?" echoed Tom. "A trilby hat, a nice check sports coat, a nice pair of brogue shoes, and a pair of cavalry twill trousers, usually an open necked shirt, and of course a strong looking sunburned chest. I've definitely got the last one" said Tom.

How they laughed together.

"Do you know?" said Kathy teasing, "that Tom made them laugh so much that Auntie Liz wet herself."

"Thomas, really" said mother.

"Well she never complained" replied Tom, "all I noticed was that Uncle Joe was wiping the tears from his eyes, with his handkerchief as they laughed. Oh yes, Dad you've missed an item out of a farmer's uniform."

"Sorry old son, what was that?"

"A red spotted handkerchief" replied Tom. "As soon as I've finished painting, I'll see how much uniform I've got" he said, "I must have most of it."

"Look" suggested father, "after tea tomorrow, we'll all go over and you can help again."

"Yippee," shouted Tom, "and do you know" he continued, "that nine piglets were born tonight while we were there. I managed to save two from being lain on, because old uncle couldn't get into the sty quick enough. So I jumped over the gate and did it for him. Tomorrow then, we'll get the car out, come to think of it, it will be out already because it's mother's shopping day. Then Sunday it's church, and visit Kathy's mum in the hospital. It will be best if we go to church in the morning because we might be late home and miss evening service.''

Tom learns to be a farmer

CHAPTER 4

Next morning Tom pressed two one pound notes into Kathy's hand, very secretly saying, "Shush".

While they were having breakfast, Mrs Monkton said "Would you like to come shopping with me Kathy, only if you want to mind?"

Kathy looked at Tom, who just winked back. "Yes I'll come" replied Kathy.

"Let me see now, father wants to go out for an hour or two."

Just then father caught Tom's eye, he winked, Tom just nodded back, mother saw all this. As they finished breakfast the postman called — a letter for Kathy — she opened it eagerly.

"It's from Mum," she said. "Oh Tom, she can get out of bed already. Auntie Gretchen I'm so thrilled."

She handed the letter to Mrs Monkton, who read it saying , "Yes they have started to get her out of bed for a while each day, and on Monday the doctor is going to take the stitches out. Oh my, she is doing well. I suppose you've got all the bills, Frank?"

"Probably but mine can wait, I must be off now anyway, are you coming Tom?"

"Yeah could do," he replied casually — off they went.

Tom squeezed Kathy's hand as he passed her chair.

Out came the car, and off they went; father and Tom; yes of course straight over to Bournend Farm.

When they arrived Uncle Joe was still trying to milk the cows. He had finished one and was about to start on the other.

"Hello!" he said "what's all this then."

"We just popped over to have a word Uncle Joe."

"Here give me the stool" said Mr Monkton.

He settled under the cow and was soon pulling out goodly streams of milk.

Tom watched fascinated, then he crept closer saying, "Show me

Dad." Which he did. Much to father's surprise, he soon acquired the knack.

Then he stood back to let his father finish the cow off. Tom went to the head of the stalls, undid the cow chains, hung them on a nail like Uncle Joe did and turned the cows out. They went straight out to the paddock on their own, so he shut the gate and followed the two men back to the house.

Auntie Liz greeted them and said, "You haven't even had your breakfast yet I suppose, Frank?"

"Yes Auntie, we are both OK."

"I've cooked uncle's. Now, will you have a cup of tea?"

"Yes we wouldn't say no to that."

After Tom had helped auntie with the cups and things for the table, they all sat down.

"Now then Thomas, how's that little gal?" asked Uncle Joe.

"She's just fine" replied Tom, "she had a letter from her mum this morning, and she has started to get out of bed already."

"That's quick" said Auntie Liz.

"Yes but they get them moving quicker these days," suggested Mr Monkton.

As Uncle Joe tucked into his eggs and bacon, Tom's father said "Now Uncle Joe what about this tough young farmer here?"

Joe looked up now, becoming a bit bemused, "Oh yes Frank, I see."

Both men exchanged a wink.

"Now" said Joe "I'll tell you my side of it. I want him here because he's a real Monkton, you see Frank I want a real Monkton to take this on. What's your side of it then Frank?"

"Same as yours I reckon Uncle Joe, and what's your side of it then Tom?"

"Well the palms of my hands are itching and there is only way to stop that, get cracking on some work."

"OK Tom as soon as you are free, come on over."

"I hope to finish Kathy's house on Wednesday" answered Tom, "then I'll be here. Now while I'm here, is there anything I can do for you?"

"Yes I've only got to feed the hens, I have let them out. Give them one small bucket of corn, it's all in the corn bin, bucket as well. Throw it about well, mind, otherwise some don't get any."

Tom was gone like a shot.

While he was away, Uncle Joe told father about Tom and about his sheep up on the downs in a thunderstorm. "My sides fair ached this morning, through laughing at him. Mind you, he jumped into the pigsties and managed to get two piglets out from under the old

D

sow and I've still got all nine of 'em. When he realised that I needed help here badly, he placed his feet apart, shoved his hands down into his trouser pockets, stuck out his chin, then he said 'Right Uncle Joe you need a farmer, then I'm your man.' Now that Frank, is a real Monkton. My God I was that pleased with the lad, I shall also take care of him, no need to worry Frank. I don't know how all this came about, but he's the answer to my prayers.''

The two men shook hands.

"I'll come over and show him things as well Uncle Joe.''

"Thanks very much Frank, some things I'll have a job to show him owing to my leg.''

Tom was coming back now.

"Everything OK out there Tom?''

"Yes, and I've put some clean straw in some of the nest boxes — an egg or two has been broken in them you see.''

"Good man, good man,'' replied Uncle Joe.

Tom started to help auntie, who asked him when she was going to see that little girl again.

"Oh very soon Auntie Liz. Do you really like her?''

"I should jolly well think I do. She's a real treasure. You see Tom, she's so sensible, and she knows how to set about a job.''

"Yes I've noticed'' replied Tom. "One day she'll make me a good farmer's wife, when she's ready of course.''

How Auntie Liz laughed at him. "I'm glad you've got it all organized Tom,'' she said. "Does she know yet?''

"Oh yes,'' replied Tom, "she's known for several years.''

"Oh Tom, you are a proper caution.''

Father came now saying, "Come on old sunshine, there's work to do.''

Off they went to the big barn. Father opened the door, there stood a tractor.

"Is that it?'' asked Tom.

"Yep,'' replied father.

Tom was looking all around it.

"Right'' said father, "now to start her up. Remember she starts on petrol then when she's warm you switch over to paraffin. Now watch closely Tom — first you open this drain cock here, to make sure there is no paraffin in the carburettor — then shut it. This tank here is for petrol only, it is written on the cap here, look, and this is the petrol tap for this tank. This tank here is for TVO only — that's paraffin really — TVO stands for Tractor Vapourizing Oil, and here is the tap for this tank. This big one here in front is of course your radiator, it's for water only, of course.''

"Yep," said Tom, "petrol, paraffin, water, drain cock for the carburettor."

"Good, now start her up. Petrol on, retard this lever up to half-way, it's your magneto, pull out this, it's your choke, now crank her up."

After three pulls she started, "Now" shouted father "push your choke in to half-way, put your mag lever back to its running position, so."

Then father jumped up, put the tractor into reverse and backed it out of the barn. Tom followed him out, then father showed him how to switch off the petrol and to open the TVO tap as the engine was warm enough now.

"Jump up" said father, "I'm going to show you the farm; also watch closely, how I drive this monster."

Tom was eager as a young hawk. Off they went.

Father pointed out this field, and that crop, and so on, until they came to the top of the track, where a gate opened on to the open downs.

"And now Master Thomas, you can try your luck out here."

"Can I?" asked Tom.

"Yes you've got to use this tool so come on."

Father explained the tractor twice, remembering that Tom could already drive the van quite reasonably. Tom asked a few questions to make sure, then he tried his luck. He was a bit jerky at first to start with, but he soon mastered that, and enjoyed a good drive round. Back into the farm track now, where father shut the gate, off they went and were soon back in the barn. Tom now had to stop the engine, he turned off the TVO. After a while the engine stopped. They closed the barn doors now. As they crossed the yard Uncle Joe met them.

"Just a little practice, and he's your farmer Uncle Joe."

"We can easily arrange that Frank," he replied.

"Now we've got a painting job on Uncle Joe, and we'll see you Monday evening at the latest."

"OK men" said uncle, as they left shouting their 'goodbyes'.

On the way home, father told Tom that he would be showing him most of the jobs to help ease Uncle Joe's problem of not being able to get about.

"We'll milk Monday evening," said father, "then perhaps on Tuesday evening we'll see if you can do it yourself. I think you will soon master the whole job, we'll talk about it at home. So ask all the questions you can think of, it don't matter if they do seem a bit daft, it's a good way to learn."

"Dad, there is one question," said Tom, "how do you know all this? You know all about the farm, how to do this and that job."

Father just laughed, "I was brought up over there as a youngster, I just wouldn't be anywhere else. Then after the war my dad left me the builder's business, and here we all are. You see son, you were born at Bournend Farm, so really you are only going back home every time you go there. We are only here because grandad left me our place of course. Uncle Joe owns two cottages, they belong to the farm for farm workers."

"Then why don't he get some workers in?" asked Tom.

"Good question" replied father, one cottage is condemned; it's got to be renovated before it's habitable, in fact one end must be rebuilt. The other houses his last workman, old Tom Marshall. He's got a bad heart now and can't be moved. Uncle Joe would never ever try to get him out, Joe would consider it cruel to even ask him to leave. You see he's lived there for years and years and he's given faithful service all through, so of course, Joe is simply letting him die there."

Tom looked very sad, then he said about doing up the other cottage.

"Yes Joe, has only just got permission from the council to do it his way, which is to enlarge it. I've got the contract when Joe says so."

"Let's see if the ladies are home yet, it's twelve-thirty now."

As they went into the house, mother shouted, "It's ready when you are boys."

The boys, as mother called them, washed their hands ready to eat.

"It's faggots, peas and chips," said Kathy, who seemed to be very busy. She helped to dish it up, then gave Tom a small parcel. "It's a present for a farmer," she said sitting down beside him.

After putting some chips into his mouth, Tom opened it. It was three lovely, big red spotted handkerchiefs, and a real nice leather belt.

"Just what I always wanted," he said, "Now I can muck out the pigs, oh 'arrh, and the chicken, and wean the calves me dearee' oh." Then he gave Kathy a kiss and ate his meal quite ravenously. "Ya' know," he said, "us tractor drivers just got to wear a good belt, otherwise it shakes your 'innards', riding all day without it; ya' see you would go bow-legged, that's what" he announced.

They laughed at Tom as he said, " 'Twas only this mornin, I was drivin up thro' the 'varm', when I lost one of me back wheels. Good job I had a spare on me watch chain."

How they laughed at Tom's droll way of putting things.

"I'm sure we shall hear some funny tales about farming from now on," said mother.

"Well, now if you've had enough Tom, we got some painting to do for Kathy."

"Have we?" asked Tom.

"Yes us farmers must stick together" replied father.

"Yes sir," shouted Tom realizing what his father meant. Up he got saying "Come on Dad, don't hang about there's work to do.

Mother and Kathy laughingly watched them go.

At number six, they stripped for work, overalls on.

"Now just where have you got to?" asked father.

Tom showed him.

"This sitting-room is a pretty good job. Not bad at all old son."

"Only the skirting-board to finish in here, and I've done the passage ceiling and the kitchen ceiling twice. I did wash it" said Tom.

"OK, you finish the sitting-room, and I'll start on the passage walls" replied father, "then we can finish the kitchen walls together."

"Bang on" agreed Tom, as he piled into the work.

After about an hour Tom had completely finished the sitting-room. He went into the passage to see father. He was very surprised to see that it was almost finished.

"Another half-hour old son."

"Looks smashing old daddie," he replied. "Yep, looks real good for a learner."

"Cheeky young devil," said father not stopping for even one second.

Tom started on the kitchen walls working with great gusto, and singing 'To be a Farmer's Boy'. This was followed by 'Good Old Sussex by the Sea'.

As he finished his song, there was great clapping and shouts of 'more', 'more' and 'hear', 'hear'. Mother, Kathy and Pastor Jones were standing there.

Tom stood up, bowed politely and said, "I'm glad you appreciate a good voice, thank you my friends."

"We've brought some lubrication for your tonsils dear boy," replied mother. "But we only brought it after you explained that painters have to drink lots of tea, and eat lots of fruit cake or they will get painter's colic; so I thought it time for a tea-break."

"Oh Thomas," said Pastor Jones, "you never said that to your mother?"

"Ah, yes, well" replied Thomas, "it could be right, you know."

"I doubt it" replied Pastor Jones.

"Ah well," replied Tom, tucking into a large slice of cake, "it's not been disproved."

"Well I'll give you the benefit of the doubt then," said Pastor Jones laughing.

"Knew you'd see it my way" agreed Tom, who was now on his second piece of cake.

"Tom really," Kathy was saying, "it takes me all my time to keep up pouring the tea for you, where do you put it?"

"It's the inner man," Tom was telling her. "Take a car for instance, if you don't keep pouring in the petrol it stops, men are just the same" he explained.

Everyone was sniggering at Tom's remark.

"I hear you intend to become a rich farmer" said Pastor Jones.

"True" replied Tom, "very true. Do you know" said Tom, in between mouthfuls of cake, "my great grandfather, who was incidently named after me. Did you know he came here penniless? In the spring he sowed three rows of peas in his garden. But the very next morning he became quite down-hearted, he almost despaired, as he looked out of his bedroom window, he cried, 'Woe is me,' because there was a big cock pheasant eating all his peas. It had scratched up the rows and eaten them all. Now my friends, his very life depended on the pea crop; with a name like Tom Monkton, he was of course a very resourceful man, and with a name like Tom, well I mean. So he crept downstairs, loaded his gun and shot the pheasant dead. Bang!"

"Oh no," cried the ladies.

"Yep," replied Tom, "then he noticed how big the pheasant's crop was with all the peas he had eaten. So he whipped out his knife, cut his crop open and tipped out all the peas, ya' know what happened then? Well he resowed the peas and cooked the pheasant for his dinner, now he had a marvellous crop of peas and he's never looked back."

Everyone present just fell about laughing, fit to burst absolutely helpless they were. While Tom still ate his cake with a straight solemn face, just staring at the others. Poor old Pastor Jones, was drying his eyes now and still laughing.

"My word, Tom," he said, "if you can farm as well as you can tell yarns, you will be big success."

"That," replied Tom "coming from you, and you being a 'bestest' pal, of mine. You are definitely right. What was it you said?"

"Oh I can't remember now" he replied still laughing.

"Well just to bring it back to your mind," said Tom, "listen to this. One evening in the winter, my great grandad was going home from work with his gun tied on the cross bar of his bike. *Honest,* said Tom, "when he passed by the barn of a neighbouring farmer and there scratching for his supper beside the barn was a big fat cock pheasant. But my dear old grandad was crafty, he rode on past the barn making out that he never saw the bird. Then when he was out of sight of the pheasant, in the gathering gloom, he stopped, jumped off his bike, took his gun, then crouching low he ran like . . ."

"Tom!" shouted mother.

"Like I was saying" continued Tom, "crouching low, he ran like the wind, up the side of the barn and around the far end. He peeped to see if the bird was still there. Yes in the gathering gloom he could still see it, scratching for it's supper. So he took a chance, bang he shot it. Quick as a deer he rushed down, picked it up and stuffed it inside his coat. Then he jumped on his bike and away like the '*wind*', Mother — now remember he hadn't eaten for weeks. As he got home, he left his bike by the wall of the house, took his gun and nipped indoors. He stood with his back to the door, breathing heavily. 'What's up?' asked his wife. 'It's all right dear,' he replied, 'I've got a nice fat cock pheasant for supper tonight.' 'Oh goody' said his wife, so he pulled out the pheasant to show her. 'Oh my g. g. goodness,' exclaimed his wife. It was the neighbouring farmer's best Rhode Island Red hen, it had escaped from the barn. 'Oh well,' he said 'it was nearly dark anyway, and it looked just like a pheasant; he won't be very pleased, I suppose'."

"You rotter!" replied father, as they all laughed.

"Where does he get it all from?" asked Pastor Jones.

"No one knows, but I'm sure he means well" said mother. "Sometimes he comes out with not too nice a saying."

"Oh dear," said Pastor Jones, "what does he say then?"

Father whispered to Pastor Jones, who immediately burst out laughing, "What speed" he remarked.

"Oh it's not so bad Thomas, all I can say is the Monktons are a real tough lot indeed."

"Indeed they are" replied Tom, who was working away on the wall.

"I'm off now, see you tomorrow," said the Pastor. "Goodbye, and goodbye to the story-telling farmer," he called.

"Nice man that," said Tom, as the painters got cracking again on the walls.

Kathy collected up the dirty dishes, washed them up and packed them into a basket. As they left, mother said, "Don't forget it's tea at five-thirty mind." It was a quarter to six when they went in, tried out — tea was ready and they ate it.

After tea Tom said, how refreshed he was. "Come on Kathy, let's go to the flicks."

Off they went hand-in-hand, with Tom dressed as a farmer, while Kathy was wearing a smart new costume that auntie had given her as a present.

Mother and father watched them going off to the flicks, as Tom calls it, hand-in-hand as usual, chatting away to each other like two little children.

"Yes they are growing up fast my dear, and I haven't noticed it I suppose. I must say though," said Mr Monkton, "I do feel sorry for his great grandad."

They both laughed at this.

"Poor old devil" said Mr Monkton. "They will come in later, tired out and starving, just like grandad. We never hear anything about great grandma."

"We might later, if Aunt Liz tells him something; anyway Pastor Jones was highly amused at Tom and his wonderful tales."

"Yes" agreed Mrs Monkton, "but I felt sure that he would forget that Pastor Jones was there when he was telling his tale and say something naughty."

"Never fear, my dear, he wouldn't do that. He was of course leading you on to think that, I could tell; he's as smart as new paint never fear."

"I suppose you are right, Frank, especially now that he's a farmer."

Mr Monkton dozed for an hour, then he went up to the attic and came back with a large book. After cleaning off the dust, he sat at the table looking through it.

"What's the book about dear?" asked his wife.

"Well" he replied, "I remembered it just now, it's called the *Practicalities of Farming from A to Z*. I thought it might help our 'red-spotted handkerchief son'. Uncle Joe gave it to me as a present, years ago, I think he saw it advertised in *The Farm, Field and Fireside* magazine. We were living at Bournend Farm at the time in the old cottage."

"Oh yes, I remember, it was when Aunt Liz gave me that lovely dinner service. Oh Frank, they were such lovely days living there! Looking back now, there was no electricity in the village then, and we used to put young Thomas to bed and leave him a night-light, just in case he cried.''

"Yes, but after all he didn't cry much" replied father. "Well only if he had tummy ache.''

"It's a wonder" replied mother, "the lad doesn't suffer from it now and cry all day with the amount of cake he eats.''

"Yes" agreed father, "but Tom is not like his great grandfather. He was so poor he had to go weeks without food, to say nothing of all the cider he used to get rid of.''

They both had a good laugh at his grandad. Then they heard shrieks of laughter coming from outside the back door.

It opened, in came the youngsters with Kathy saying, "Oh you fibber Tom, honestly.''

"Now then, Thomas what are you telling Kathy?''

"Nothing much" replied Tom, coming into the room.

"It's his dear old grannie that's caused it" said Kathy.

"Oh dear, what did she do?" asked auntie.

"You won't believe this Auntie Gretchen, but he says that his grannie used to go out on the downs and catch rabbits. He said she could run as fast as the speed of light. She used to catch lots of rabbits, chop them up and boil them until the meat came off the bones, and she used to mince the meat and fill up jam jars with it, then she would seal it in with melted fat to keep it airtight, and it would keep for weeks. She used to mix it up with mashed potatoes and fry it like rissoles. To keep her butter and milk cool, and her meat during the hot weather, she used to put it all in buckets, then lower them down the well. It was very deep, and very cold down there, it was nearly freezing, and do you know what happened after that? Well he said, that his grannie's cat was so hungry, but very resourceful, and it climbed down the rope to the bottom of the well and ate the lot. The cat was so big and heavy that it couldn't climb out. He also said, it so happened that his grannie wanted some meat, so she wound up the bucket and there was this great fat cat, blown out with all the meat it had eaten and sound asleep.''

How they all laughed and laughed.

"But that's not all" said Tom, "that very afternoon was the village flower show, so she carried her cat, still asleep mind you, and entered it for the big cat competition. It won hands down, weighing in at forty-five pounds.''

"Oh Thomas, you fibber, you big, big, fibber," said Kathy.

They all laughed and laughed.

"Let's have supper," suggested mother, "it's cold beef and pickles.''

"That was it, I knew it was something we had to do" replied Tom, "supper."

As they ate it Tom was looking through the book that father had just given him. "This is the book" announced Tom, "it's got all new inventions for the next fifty years already in it; good old Dad. You know Mum, if he was a girl, I'd kiss him."

This caused a bit of an uproar, because Tom always said things in such a droll sort of way.

Kathy helped to clear away the supper things, and to help get things ready for the morning. Then she sat with Tom, who just could not put the book down. Tom read through the article on egg production.

"It goes" explained Tom, "from a day old chick, up through the growing stages, through laying; how to clean, handle and sell and to grade eggs, so that they all look the same size ready for sale. Yes I reckon, that poultry keeping is very nice" said Tom.

"What's so very special about poultry keeping?" asked mother.

"Well," replied Tom, "if one kicked you it wouldn't hurt much."

"You big fool" said Kathy, "you honestly take the biscuit."

"It's not so much that they kick" replied father, "but peck. Your Uncle Joe used to have those big Marans; they lay a lovely big appetizing looking egg; very dark brown almost a red colour; they sell like hot cakes. One of the cockerels would even chase the old sheepdog away from the hens."

"Yes.s.s, I remember" said Tom, "he chased the sheepdog so badly one day, that it ran away and never came back. You can remember surely, Dad? and for punishment" continued Tom, "old Uncle Joe made him round up the sheep. He made hundreds of pounds out of it."

"Oh my goodness," laughed Mr Monkton, "I wish I hadn't started this."

Tom carried on reading as though nothing had happened.

Mrs Monkton said, "Mind you Kathy, going back to what you were talking about when you came in, that bit about preserving rabbit meat is quite true. Also that it's very cool down a well in summer. The older people did put their things down a well to keep it."

"Honestly Mum," said Tom, "do I ever tell fibs?"

"Yes" replied mother, "sometimes."

"What's your favourite type of farming dad?" asked Tom.

"Sheep, poultry and growing crops" replied father, "that is what I would do if I had Uncle Joe's farm. You see you need the least amount of capital to start with. Your sheep are your travelling 'dung-carts'; they dung the land for you as you pen them over the fields. Now your chickens, which is only a sideline, they are fed on your tail corn, or seconds, which is blown out when you thresh your corn ricks. I look at it like this, the work is spread over the year evenly, starting after Christmas. The first thing that happens after Christmas, you get your lambs. This must be so for several reasons, which I won't go into here and now. By the time you can safely leave them, it's corn sowing time; then you can manage along nicely, making a little hay for your house cows, and some for the sheep, not too much; then it's harvest time. Now your chickens are easily managed during the year at anytime, but between harvest and Christmas, or even after, you can thresh out your corn ricks and sell your corn. That's the type of farming I like.''

All this time Tom sat listening mouth open. "How many men would you require?" asked Tom.

"Not half as many as you would need on a mixed farm. You could of course have pigs or fatten cattle, in the place of sheep. One man, you see, can normally handle sheep, chicken, a house cow and do the field work."

"I see" said Tom, "how many sheep would be required to do that type of farming on Uncle Joe's farm?"

"Well it's not a big farm, start with fifty, or work your way up to that from a dozen or so; you'll soon know how many. Now it's eighty-five acres over there, almost a one-man band, with occasional help. Look son, when you get over there. I'll come to help on any job, or anytime. Now you have a good think, then we'll talk again after awhile. That book can help you a lot. I'm for bed, I feel rather tired tonight," said father.

"Me as well" agreed Tom.

As they went to bed tired out, Tom was heard to say, "Arable and sheep farming." He gave his mum a goodnight kiss, also Kathy, saying "Goodnight Mum; goodnight farmer's wife; and goodnight dear old Dad."

Next day after a good Sunday breakfast, the family got ready for church. They all walked along to the little Methodist church. Kathy and Tom, followed by Mr and Mrs Monkton, all looking smart and neat. Pastor Jones greeted them at the door.

After the service as they came out, Pastor Jones was talking to father and mother. As Tom and Kathy walked by Tom said, "Nice sermon and thanks for those good old rousing hymns" to Pastor Jones.

"I'm glad you liked them Thomas," he replied, "by the way your father has something to tell you. I do hope you won't let me down, mind."

"You know me sir," replied Thomas grinning. They all went off home.

The Sunday lunch was cooked — it only had to be reheated. When they eventually sat down to their meal, father told Tom just what Pastor Jones wanted him to do.

He said, "As you may know, Lady Rossington, who lives in the big manor house above the village at Stonedene holds a village flower show yearly in her park. There will be the usual various sports, handicrafts, exhibitions, and so on. But this year they are trying to organize a biggest fibber contest. Now Tom, this is where you come in, Pastor Jones wants you to enter on his behalf as the prize money goes to the upkeep of the church. You see, her ladyship is a Methodist and a Liberal. Now, if you could think up something to enter the contest with, who knows, you could win. Trouble is you have only got one week, it's next Saturday. Uncle Joe and Aunt Liz will be there, I shall run them up to the park in the car."

"But Dad" protested Tom, "you know I never tell fibs."

"See what I mean" said father.

After they had finished their meal, the ladies washed up and the men went to get the car out. Tom backed it out and drove it around to the door like a real professional, watched by father, who noted every move.

"Good driving son," he said as he took the wheel.

Off they went to the hospital to see Kathy's mother.

When they arrived Kathy and Mrs Monkton went in — only two visitors at a time was the rule. They took in her clothes, fruit, cakes, and some sweets.

When at last they came out, Kathy was beaming with happiness. "She can stand up and walk a little already, she even showed us" said Kathy.

"My word, this is good news" said father.

"Yes and the doctor says about ten more days, then she should be strong enough to go home."

"Yes she really is looking wonderfully well" agreed mother.

"Now then" suggested father, "I vote we go home, get some bits and pieces, and go over to the farm and have tea with them."

Everyone agreed that this would be a nice thing to do. It would help to lighten the old people's load, and to brighten their day.

As soon as they arrived home Tom changed his clothes. The ladies took goodies and things for Auntie Liz. As they arrived at Bournend Farm, they saw Uncle Joe just toddling across the yard to fetch in the cows. Tom saw this, so he ran over to the gate calling, like Uncle Joe, "Caaaake come 'oon," he called.

The cows stopped grazing and came running up to Tom mooing. He took them into the cow pen and chained them up. He gave them their cake — one dipper, full of dairy cubes, just as he had seen Uncle Joe do. He fetched the buckets and stool; washed off the cows udders first, then he sat down to milk. After a few pulls, the cow who was happy eating her cubes, let down her milk. Tom was able to carry on milking reasonably well. Father and Uncle Joe watched from a distance. Tom changed cows and started to milk the other, continuing until he could get no more milk.

"Good man" said Uncle Joe, "now we'll just see how much you left in because the cows will dry up if they are not milked out cleanly. It's nature's way," said uncle.

Father got none from the first cow, and just a little from the second.

"Well done Tom, well done indeed" said both men.

"I feel that I've got me a good farmer here," said uncle. "I know he can handle the fowls."

Tom turned the cows out to their paddock. After shutting the gate securely, he set off for the chicken houses, while the two men went back to the house with the pail of milk.

After awhile, Tom, whistling, came back to the house with a bucketful of eggs. "Uncle Joe," he called, "you haven't fed the pigs yet."

"Frank, I'm being told off already," he said laughing. Then he shouted back, "Leave it Tom, I want to show you what to give them. We'll do it after tea."

"Good O," shouted Tom, as he now washed his hands.

Uncle Joe and Auntie Liz were overjoyed at having the family call on them. They enjoyed a lovely tea of beef and lamb sandwiches made by Kathy, with of course some of great aunt's home-made butter; then came tinned pears, with home-made clotted cream; fruit cake; apple cake; and lots of fairy cakes with cherries on top.

"You just can't beat being a farmer" said Tom. "Plenty of good food."

Yes, everyone had a most enjoyable tea-time that Sunday.

Great Aunt Liz said, "This is really like old times Gretchen. You know, I do like to see you all at anytime."

After tea, the menfolk went out to the pigs.

"How many have you got Uncle Joe?" asked Tom.

"Well, I keep as a permanent basis, eight sows and the old boar pig. Now what I do, is this."

Father took the bucket half filled it with water. He added one dipper full of meal, then stirred up the mixture until it was well-mixed, with a stick kept specially for the job. Now when mixed like that, he put one bucket of mix to each pigsty — even to the old boar. Now the piglets got theirs separate. Milk first then he topped up the bucket to half full with water; then stirred in half a dipper of meal. "That makes it thinner and you'll find that the piglets do better with the milk in it" he said. Father showed Tom how to feed the pigs by pouring their feed into their troughs.

Tom tried one and was told 'That's it, you've got it'. So he carried on while the pigs squealed and screamed for their food.

At last all finished — no more squealing — the only sounds were satisfied grunts from the happy pigs.

As they all stood looking at the pigs, Uncle Joe told Tom that every six weeks he had a litter of pigs born.

Tom was working something out in his head and looking so very intelligent about it all. "Yes" he replied "I get it."

Later that evening, Tom showed Kathy all around the farm — the pigs; the chickens; the cow pens; and Uncle Joe's young store cattle out in the pasture; the big field of dredge corn that uncle grew for cattle feed. He also grew wheat and barley to thresh out and sell, plus a small field of oats.

At last they were up on the downs, at the far end of the farm. They strolled back looking at the apples growing in the orchard. They could see the beehives with lots of bees going in and out in the evening sunshine.

"Oh Tom," said Kathy, "how I just love this farm. I could spend my whole life here with you. Yes I do love it Tom — all the animals around you; the smell of the farmyard."

They lingered for awhile taking it all in. Then they went indoors.

Great aunt Liz said "Here comes my very own favourite son and daughter. Have you had a nice stroll dears?"

"Yes, it's so lovely out there on the farm; all the animals around you; the crops growing; the smell of the farm; the birds chattering. Oh yes Auntie, it's all so wonderful. I know I shall dream about it tonight, I do hope so."

"It seems as though you like it my dear," said Uncle Joe.

"Yes I like it so much, it's like being in paradise."

"Well from both of us, come over and see us whenever you like.

You will be most welcome."

"Yes indeed" agreed Auntie Liz.

After supper, the family said 'goodbye' and went home. The ladies had arranged to have a baking day on the following Thursday, ready for the flower show on the Saturday. Kathy wanted to enter a fruit cake with almonds on top, this year; Auntie Gretchen her usual apple cake.

"I'll tell you how to win," said Tom, "and I mean this Kathy. Just put in your cake the juice of two oranges. Us farmers knows a thing or two" he said.

Kathy looked at auntie but she simply said, "We'll try one first dear, then we'll decide, it might just work."

They all sat chatting now. Tom and Kathy sat on the settee, mother and father occupied the two easy chairs. Tom became strangely silent — there he sat staring at his shoes. He seemed to be miles away, holding one of Kathy's hands between his.

"Got a problem son?" asked his father, as everyone noticed him seemingly in deep thought.

He didn't move or answer.

After a while he suddenly jumped up shouting, "Got it. Farmer's wife," he said to Kathy, "I've got it." He ran off to his room and came back with a pad.

"Have you still got it?" asked father.

"Sure, can I use your soldering iron?" he asked. "Just a small job ya' know. Oh yes can you solder silver paper?" he asked.

"I doubt it" replied father, "you can but try."

Then Tom was drawing diagrams on the paper. "Ha, ha, blooming ha," he said. "Now everyone listen to this announcement. I shall without doubt win the fibber contest. No ifs. No buts, and I'll do it without telling a fib. That's £15 for Pastor Jones."

"But" said father, "Pastor Jones expects £20."

"Yes but you see Dad — my overheads."

They laughed at Tom.

"I see" replied father, "so you want to make a business out of fibbing?"

"I've just told you Dad, I don't tell fibs, and I'll prove it at the fibbers contest."

How they laughed.

"By the way" said Tom, "I'll bet anybody here half a crown that I won't tell fibs to win the contest, and I'll prove it when I tell my fib."

They were all howling with laughter now.

"OK you are on," replied father, "how can I lose. I'll bet you your half-crown."

"And so will I" said mother.

"That's five bob we've got to come already Kathy. We shall soon cover our costs. Get as many as you like to bet on me."

"I can't see how you can win" replied father.

"My bet is that I will prove my fib to be true as soon as I've told it."

"OK" agreed father, "I'll bet you alright."

"Hee, hee, hee" chuckled Tom.

The next day he was at number six, just as soon as he had eaten his breakfast. The ceiling looked good — that didn't need another coat. Two walls, the windows, behind the back door, and the skirting boards. Because father had helped, it would now soon be finished. 'Walls first' he thought.

He had just finished this when Kathy arrived with his break; a flask of tea and some cake. After this he helped her arrange the sitting-room chairs, and things; how pleased she was.

"Have you told your mum yet?" he asked.

"No I want it to be a big surprise" she told him, "don't you think it's best that way?"

"Yeah, surprised people are nice to watch," replied Tom.

"Pleasant surprises I mean. You silly old thing Tom" she said. "When can I lay out the kitchen?"

"After tea" he told her.

"Coo, that's quick" she replied.

"Yep, I shall finish by dinner time, then I must do a bit of shopping."

"What for?" asked Kathy.

"Well for the things I shall need to tell my truthful lie with, that's what," replied Tom.

By twelve-thirty, Tom had finished. He loaded all the paint tins and tools on his wheelbarrow. He arrived home singing 'Cockles and Mussels', just as his father was about to go indoors.

"Finished then painter?" asked father.

"Yep," he told father, "and I reckon the chap who did it done a darned good job."

"Good man is he?" asked father.

"I've never seen better" replied Tom.

Father laughed saying "You'll do old son, you'll do indeed."

Later that afternoon, Tom went shopping to buy his bits and pieces. Out in the workshop, he set to and did his soldering. He couldn't solder silver paper, but he could solder the thin covering of tin found on top of a tin of Players' cigarettes. When he had finished, he tried out his invention, it worked everytime. He was singing to himself, when his mother came to see if he was alright, and did he need some afternoon tea.

"Do I?" he replied. "Solderers like me get real thirsty."

"Did you do whatever it was then?" asked mother.

"Sure I did."

"Can I ask what it was?" inquired mother.

"You can, but I won't tell you. You bet me remember?"

"Very well then," replied mother, smiling to herself. "I'll try to last out until Saturday."

Tom hid his invention up in his room. Then he spent the next hour or so hoeing in Kathy's garden.

E

Evil Kitty is thrown out of the church.
Tom and Kathy inherit the farm.
Kathy's mother is well again.

CHAPTER 5

"I'm off farming," he told everyone that evening. "I shall start at seven o'clock tomorrow morning. I shall go over on the bus and come home on the quarter to five at night; that means I should be here at about five-past five."

Before supper that evening, he helped Kathy to straighten up number six. All the furniture was put in its place and the polishing done. All the laundry had been done, curtains, table-cloths, chair covers and the like was all done and neatly ironed.

Next morning Tom was up early. Kathy came down and had her breakfast with him. She kissed him goodbye and told him to take care.

"Bye farmer's wife" waved Tom, as he ran for the bus with his lunch bag over his shoulder.

All day, Kathy, mother, and dad at lunch-time, wondered how he was doing. They watched for him to come up the road around five o'clock time. It was just after five when he came striding along humming to himself.

"Howdy partner" he greeted them.

As they ate their meal they all wanted to know how he had got on.

"OK I suppose," replied Tom. "After milking and feeding round, I cleaned out the pigs. I used the tractor and trailer and hauled the dung up to the hay field and put it in the dung clamp just inside the gate. Uncle Joe said, 'Don't hit the gate post son', I didn't. Then in the afternoon I milked the cows, fed the pigs and chickens and so on. Then about half-past four they said, 'Mustn't miss the bus mind or mother will get worried'."

Tom seemed very happy and stayed happy, with Kathy talking to him about farming every night.

"Dad, yesterday, Uncle Joe went to market with four bacon pigs. You took him in with the car and trailer. Now he had to take the best money he could get from the highest bidder of course. Now out of that money he had to take the cost of rearing the pigs, transport to market and the auctioneer's fees. I don't know what that comes to, but it must be quite a bit. Now why can't Uncle Joe breed pigs for a firm like Shippams in Chichester, or for a pork pie firm on a regular contract basis. If he did wouldn't he do better?"

Everyone was looking at Tom.

"That my son" replied father, "is a darned good question. The best thing to do is to get it down on paper. Say the cost of six pigs reared and sold in market, and for six pigs reared on contract — you would have to guess the costs roughly."

"Well, I'm only asking" replied Tom, "because Uncle Joe said 'Markets my lad, is either pennies or pounds'. Only you see Dad, I thought that by rearing pigs under contract you would have a guaranteed market."

"Yes, son, I would think you are dead right. But you must also remember that Uncle Joe is an old dyed in the wool old timer. He just loves going to market. He will never change his ways."

"Oh I do see that" agreed Tom, "I'm only asking in order to learn for myself."

"Good man," said father, "in fact that really is a darned good question. Even without checking I think you are right; a contract would be best. The buyer would come, look at our pigs; decide when he wanted them; tell you their value; send his lorry to collect on the day — job finished. The cheque gets sent to you from the firm."

On Saturday morning Tom set off for work. Dad came later with the ladies, plus a car full of items to enter in the competitions, including Tom's suitcase.

Tom had finished his jobs by the time the car arrived.

After dinner everyone went up to the park with their exhibits. As the village folk gathered, Tom slipped into the crowd. He found Kathy and mother who were watching a certain tent where the cakes were on show. After awhile the judges left, off they hurried to see if they had been awarded a prize.

"Auntie Gretchen, look, what does it mean?" she asked.

On Kathy's card was written First Prize, and highly recommended. She jumped for joy, kissing auntie.

"And me," said Tom who was acting the fool. So she kissed him as well.

Auntie was so pleased for Kathy, she went along now to see her own entry had fared. First in its class, highly recommended was also written on it. How pleased and proud they were.

"Told you," said Tom. "Uncle Joe had a first for honey, for both thick and thin. Auntie Liz had first for her home-made butter; a second for cream; and a first for her chutney."

"Oh boy," said Mrs Monkton, "our family is doing well today. There is only Tom to do his turn now."

Later in the afternoon the fibber contest started. The judges who sat in the front row were her Ladyship, and the local publican, Mr Hayward; Pastor Jones was close at hand.

It was all started off by Mr Hayward — each contestant was listened to very carefully and given many marks by the judges. They were clapped well afterwards. There was quite a good audience. At last Tom's turn came. He was the youngest contestant and the last to go. They clapped him well as he took the stand.

"Well folks," he said. "You clapped me as a young liar, or to put it more tastefully a young fibber. But believe me" he said, "I don't tell fibs."

They all laughed at this. "I'll prove it then. Now it all started years and years ago with my great grandaddy. A hard working chap indeed, I suppose," he said reflectively, "he turns after me." More sniggering. "He was coming home from work one evening when he saw an old man that he knew. 'Tom' shouted the old man, 'I want a word.' So of course grandad stopped. 'Now Tom, I've been wanting to see you for a day or two, you see I've got a big Sennan nanny-goat. I want to give her away. I'm too old now and too stiff to handle her, so I thought maybe I could give her to you. She gives three pints of milk each day. I've got a chain and collar. Now if you come up on Sunday morning you could walk her home. I know you will look after her. Her name is 'Dolly'. 'Yes thanks', said grandad 'I'll have her'. Off he went wondering where he could keep his goat. In the allotment he thought, but when he fetched the goat there was no iron peg to peg the goat chain into the ground with. So for now he put her in the allotment shed. He would carry food to her. Now he found the hurricane lantern a bit of a nuisance, so he decided to fix up an electric light. He bought a battery, a bulb, a switch and a length of flex. He fitted the battery into a wooden box, which he screwed to the wall; then he ran his flex up to a switch; then up to the bulb which he fixed to the ceiling — it all worked quite well. The next night he came home from work, he didn't hurry, he had his electric light so he didn't care. After tea he went to milk the goat, he put his hand around the door post feeling for the switch. He couldn't find it. He struck a match, nothing anywhere, so he swore a bit and fetched his lantern.

Lighting this he went in, nothing anywhere. The goat had eaten the box, the battery, the flex, switch the bulb holder, the lot. Grandad was utterly amazed, but he milked his goat, went home drunk the milk — of course it tasted good. Now friends, to prove that I wasn't telling fibs, as some of you might secretly think, this is what happened to him. For ever after that, the electricity from the battery got into the goat's milk; then it got into grandad's blood and it has been passed on even down to me. You see every time we need a torch we don't even have to buy one, we just take a bulb from our pockets like so," said Tom holding a torch bulb in his left hand, "then we pass it into our right hand so, and hey presto.The bulb lights up." And the bulb did light up. He made sure it was seen by all. Then he did it once again, saying "There you are my friends, that proves that my fib was the truth." Then he walked off to join Kathy.

Oh how they clapped, cheered and whistled.

"Told you" he said to his folks.

"I don't know what you are going to do next," said Uncle Joe, giving him a slap on the back. Her Ladyship was now consulting with her advisors.

"Her Ladyship will speak" shouted Mr Hayward — all went quiet.

"Well" she said, "the fibber contest seems to be going well, all were good contestants. However, after hearing them all we have come to a unanimous conclusion; the last contestant wins hands down, and I must add I really did enjoy it."

They all clapped and cheered as Tom went up for his prize, which he handed over right away to Pastor Jones, "For my 'bestest' pal" he said.

How they laughed at Tom and clapped him. Her Ladyship told Tom it was one of the best stories she had ever heard.

"Where did you get it from?" she asked.

"I make them up" replied Tom.

"Well you certainly know how to put them over." Then catching sight of Uncle Joe, she said, "Now Joe Monkton, it's not you that's been teaching this young man, is it?"

"No Milady, he's a young Monkton that's how it is."

"Joe you are incorrigible. Now how's that leg of yours?"

"Well it never gets any better Ma'am, but now I'm seventy-eight, I don't suppose it will."

"Joe Monkton you are as tough as an old boot," replied her Ladyship. "Now when you have had enough, come and see me I shall be only too willing to buy you out."

"No chance of me ever selling" replied Joe.

"I think you will eventually," she said. "You know where I live.
With that, she went off towards the WI tent.

Tom told Kathy that he must soon go to milk the cows.

"Can I come Tom? I'll be good if you'll let me watch," she said.
"Let me come, please."

"OK but we must tell Mum."

They found mother with the rest of the family at the coconut
shies. Father had two coconuts and was trying again. He managed
one more, "Oh dear, that's all I can throw now," he said, "my
arm."

Tom announced that it was time for him to milk, and that Kathy
wanted to come as well.

Aunt Liz said "Here take the back door key. You'll find some
overalls in the kitchen, it will help to keep you clean."

Off they hurried down to the park gate and along the road to the
farm.

In the kitchen Tom put his overalls on, discarding his jacket.
While Kathy did as she was told and slipped on one of auntie's
overalls over her dress.

Off they went to the paddock gate.

Tom shouted "Caaake come ooon."

The cows came running up giving a good moo. Over they went
into the cow pen, no trouble at all, knowing they would get their
dairy cubes. Tom chained them up, fed them, and fetched his stool
and bucket. While they ate their cake, Tom set to and milked both
cows, watched closely by Kathy.

"One day Tom, could I try milking?" she asked.

"Yep, why not" agreed Tom, "then when I have to go to
market, you can milk the cows. Just talk to them like I do. Uncle
Joe says if you talk to animals they listen to you, and are less likely
to mess about. These two cows are called Daisy and Buttercup."

Tom carried the pail of milk into the larder, then off to let the
cows graze in the paddock by the stream.

"Now it's the hens," he said.

Off they went. Tom was showing Kathy how much corn to give
them, and to throw it about well and evenly. While the hens rushed
about pecking up their corn, they went to pick up the eggs. Kathy
was amazed at the amount of eggs they picked up — they filled the
bucket. She couldn't carry them, so she caught hold of the bucket
to help Tom. They carried them back to the house.

"Now the pigs" said Tom.

Up they went to the pigsties. As soon as Tom touched the bucket, they all started squealing for their tea. Tom showed Kathy how they were fed. At last the squealing stopped; all fed, they had a quick look round, all seemed well.

"That's it, my little farmer's wife," he said.

"Thanks for letting me come Tom, I did enjoy myself, honestly. It's funny, but I just love it here, it seems such a happy place."

As they neared the house, a boy of about twelve and his sister, saw them crossing the yard. These two children went to the same school in town. They were called John and Sally.

They rode into the yard on their bikes.

"Hello!" they said, "we've heard things about you two."

"What things?" demanded Tom.

"Well, your Aunt Kitty told mum that you had got Kathy into trouble, and she's going to have a baby."

"Oh did she," replied Tom. "Now listen, if you don't want your ears boxed, just go home and tell your mother to come and tell that to my father, because if she doesn't you will be in trouble with the police. Now get off this property. Go on the pair of you."

Off they went.

"My God," said Tom, "wait until I tell Mum. She'll kill that big-mouthed Kitty."

"No Tom, don't make trouble."

"What on earth do you mean Kath?"

"Well two other people have asked me the same thing. They both said Kitty Monkton told them."

"Right," replied Tom taking off his overalls. "That big-mouthed Kitty Monkton will shut up, even if I have to do it with my fists."

Just then father drove into the yard with the family. He helped the old people out of the car. In they all came, Kathy had a big kettle nearly boiling, and they all sat down to a good old cup of tea.

"Now what's up with you two?" asked father.

"Not much" replied Tom.

"Hey, you haven't fell out have you?"

Pastor Jones came then, saying "I'm just longing for a cup of tea."

"Have tea and welcome," he was told.

There followed lots of chatter then about the events of the day.

"Now look Tom," said father, "what's the trouble old son? This is not like you, you know."

"Well we haven't fell out as you might think. Kathy don't want me to tell you anyway."

"Well then have you broken something."

"No" answered Kathy.

"I'll be breaking someone's darned neck more like it," replied Tom.

"Thomas," said mother, "you mustn't talk like that."

"Hold hard there," replied Tom, "you will when I tell you, so here goes."

Tom then told them in every detail, what had happened. Everyone listened in silence. Then Kathy, seeing that she couldn't hide it any longer told her story of the gossip that was getting at her.

"Now" said Tom, "I don't care what anybody thinks of me. This is a load of damn lies. Yes" he went on, "Kathy and I know all about such things, but we would never do such a thing as that. Never! We have made a pact to do everything in life proper — white wedding the lot. Having said that, what makes me hopping mad is this, there's Kathy with no dad to stand up for her; a sick mum in hospital; and now she has to do nothing, while evil people destroy her character. No I will not keep quiet. Anyone picking on Kathy, picks on me twice," added Tom. "I say, hasn't Kitty Monkton heard of the ninth commandment about gossiping and backbiting."

"Look Frank, can you enlighten me a bit more?" asked Pastor Jones.

So father explained all he could to him. How Kitty seems only to want the house and yard. He told him that her menfolk were a useless lot at work. Then he told Pastor Jones that when his father was ill, no one would look after him, or do anything for him. So of course said father, we did; but unfortunately father didn't live long after that, but he left us the house, yard, and business, as Joe here knows full well.

" 'Tis right," replied Joe, "ever since that day she has been mischief making."

Auntie Gretchen was comforting little Kathy, who was sobbing bitterly.

Pastor Jones said how Kitty Monkton always came into the back of the church about five minutes after the service had started, and left just before it finished. "But just you wait until tomorrow, I shall really sort this out."

"And so shall I," said Tom's mother.

"Good old Mum," said Tom. "Let's go down there now, and bash 'em all up. That'll teach 'em."

"Tom really," said Pastor Jones, "I do hope you will leave this to me."

"I can only say this," replied Tom, "and I mean it. If it isn't put right tomorrow, I shall do it myself. I'm not having Kathy like that."

Everyone looked at Kathy, who was still weeping in auntie's arms.

"Please don't cry," said Tom, "we all love you, honestly."

So he went and held Kathy's hand to try and comfort her.

After a while she gained control of herself and said, "I don't want you all to suffer for my sake."

"Now, now," said auntie, "the slurr is on all of us here, my dear."

Great Auntie Liz was most upset, "How could that woman be so evil" she said. "If I live to see her again, I'll slap her face good and hard."

The men were chatting away together, but Tom was still with his mother, trying to comfort Kathy.

At last she said "Thanks Auntie Gretchen, I'm alright now. You do trust us don't you auntie?"

"It has never crossed my mind that you would misbehave," replied auntie.

"Well of course, we wouldn't misbehave. How could we let everyone down? That includes my Mum and God himself." Then she started to collect up the crocks and prepared to wash them up.

Now at that moment a plan was forming in Tom's mind, "Yes" he said, "that should do the trick. Big Bessie, she will love it. But how can I get to talk to her? I know!"

So his plan to really knock this Auntie Kitty character formed in his mind. Gradually, they all got over their mighty upset — calm settled on the place once more.

Tom noticed that Kathy could even smile again, so he whispered "Nice to see you smile again, my dear little farmer's wife."

Kathy smiled and said "You are so sweet to me, my darling farmer's wife's husband."

"There you see," said Tom, "you nearly tripped up. But however you will be OK when you've been over here a bit more often."

They were laughing together now, Aunt Liz noticed.

She whispered to Kathy "You'll see some fun tomorrow, so have a good laugh for me. I never did like that woman. You'll be just fine, you'll see. Why don't you come and tell me the outcome tomorrow night?"

"Yes you bet we'll do that," agreed Tom.

At last they said their 'goodbyes', and set off for home.

F

Before they left, Tom gave Auntie Liz a note. "Give this to Uncle Joe, he'll understand." The note read *'Please Uncle Joe, can you manage to milk first thing tomorrow morning, as I have to plan to help Kathy, and I need to talk to a certain woman (not Auntie Kitt) will see you later, Tom.'*

Early next morning, Tom set off on his bike. The family thought that he was gone to the farm. But no, he went to River Road, and knocked on a certain door. After a while, the door opened and a large woman stood there tying her dressing-gown belt.

"What in the name of Joseph are you doing here at this time of day, young Thomas? I was still in bed sleeping, so I was."

"Yes I know" replied Tom, "and I really am sorry, but I do need your help very badly."

"In that case come on in, me boy'o," said Big Bessie.

Now, Bessie was a big Irish woman. She was about eighteen stone. Mr Monkton used to say that she was an all-in wrestler in disguise. Her job in life was keeping the police station clean, and looking after the single policemen's food when and where necessary. Her husband was killed in the war. She was a good churchwoman, fun loving and as honest as the day is long. They went in and sat down in Bessie's flat. Bessie put the kettle on the gas for a cup of tea, then she sat down to talk to Tom.

"Now young man, just tell your Auntie Bessie all your troubles."

Tom told her all about the troubles he had; who caused them, and why. In fact he told her everything.

She listened intently to Tom, "And this little coleen of yours, that must be the little gal that comes to church with you?"

"Yes, that's my farmer's wife," he agreed.

"Right now, just where do I come in me boy'o?"

"Well" said Tom, "I thought, do I have a good friend who could really embarrass that evil woman to such a degree that the lesson would be driven home for good. You see, I thought something like this. Like I said, she always sneaks in at the back of the church after the service has started; then I remembered Auntie Bessie. Not only would she help me, she would also help Pastor Jones and save him a very embarrassing job, and in fact she would do the whole church a favour as well. Even the whole town, and at the same time she would enjoy doing it. Now my plan went something like this. When Pastor Jones is preaching his sermon on the ninth commandment, he must come to a point where he will say something like this:— 'And verily I say unto you, cast out the evil that is among you' — now that's where you jump up and say 'Hold it, here is a most evil-tongued woman, I will cast her out.' You being sat there at the back or near at hand, then everyone looks round, you scuffle her out of the church.''

"Yes," agreed Bessie, "I see what you t'ink I ought to do." She thought for a moment then she said, "You'll get me shot boy'o."

"No fear of that" replied Tom. "We'll all jump up and cheer you on and we'll all clap like mad."

Big Bessie thought for a while. "Now I do see you have a problem not being allowed to bash 'em up. Your mum and dad like you are my good friends. Now I can't let down a friend of mine. Right," she said jumping up, "you just leave it to me, I'll fix that evil Kitty, by the saints so I will. Saint Patrick here I come."

"Auntie Bessie, you are a blooming angel. Now don't say I came to see you mind, just have a brain lapse."

"I'll be the soul of discretion, so I will" she said.

"God will bless you my Auntie Angel Bessie," replied Tom. "Hey!" he said, "if I dash off now I can still milk the cows for Uncle Joe, and get home in time for my breakfast."

So he gave Bessie a kiss and ran for it.

Uncle Joe was about to start milking, when Tom skidded into the yard.

"OK, Uncle Joe," he called, "I've made it."

"Hey, go steady young fella, you'll knock the barn over."

"I've fixed it Uncle Joe, no doubt about that. We'll tell you what happens tonight."

"Look here, now young Tom, no busting people on the nose."

"Oh no, Uncle Joe, nothing like that, something much more subtle, but very effective, hee hee hee."

"You promise me now."

"I promise Uncle Joe, even on the bible."

"Alright Tom, that's good enough for me, now I'll do the pigs while you are milking."

As soon as Tom had finished, he took in the milk, ran back to let the cows out, then over to the chickens. Now back to Uncle Joe, but he had finished the pigs.

"Thanks for helping me today uncle," he said. "Don't tell anyone, but I suppose it will come out, and when it does it will be like a big grandaddy joke."

"OK Tom, I'm looking forward to a good side-splitting joke and a good laugh tonight. Good luck old boy," he shouted, as Tom set off for home like the wind.

Uncle Joe watched him go, 'Like one of his bats out of hell', he thought. Then he shook his head and smilingly went indoors.

When Tom arrived home, Kathy said "Breakfast in ten minutes."

"OK, farmer's wife," replied Tom, as he washed his hands.

After breakfast he went to help Kathy and his mother prepare the vegetables. The ladies liked the midday meal all cooked, before they set off for church. As the morning wore on, they all set off to walk to church.

On arriving they took their seats near the front. Tom had a peep behind him, but no Auntie Bessie in sight.

'What's she up to?' he thought 'I suppose she's turned windy about it and decided not to come today.'

The service started out now; the first hymn; prayers; his father went out to read the lesson. The lesson was the *Ten Commandments*, which Mr Monkton read beautifully. Tom could not look round now.

As the service went on, Pastor Jones said, "Today we shall concentrate on the ninth commandment, thou shalt not bear false witness against thy neighbour." Pastor Jones really put it over well. "At last, under the heading of taming the tongue, we read in *James 3:7-8* 'But the tongue no man can tame. It is an unruly evil, full of deadly poison, it should be cast out as a profane evil thing indeed'."

Suddenly at the back of the church came a noise of great scuffling and screams, then someone shouted, "This is the evil in this church, begorrah. Come on you evil bitch, out you go in the name of God."

As everyone looked, Big Bessie was scuffling out evil Kitty by the scruff of the neck and the seat of the pants.

"Out you go evil Kitty until you repent," and out she jolly well went.

Back came Bessie dusting her hands to sit down once more quietly in her seat again.

Pastor Jones cleared his throat and carried on. Then came the last hymn and the blessing. As they all trooped out there was no sign of evil Kitty. Big Bessie was going on down the road in her own sweet way, speaking to this and that person as usual. Pastor Jones thanked them at the door as they left. Tom heard him say to father "When I saw what was happening I could not believe my luck. I doubt if she will ever come again, you know."

"She must have been deeply embarrassed, and it serves her jolly well right," said father.

When they arrived home and started to heat up their meal, Mrs Monkton said, "Now father what was going on at the back of the church?"

"Well" replied father, "for some reason or another Big Bessie picked up evil Kitty, and threw her out of the church, because of her evil tongue."

"Good old Bessie," cheered Tom.

Then mother looked at Tom saying, "I hope this was nothing to do with you Master Thomas."

"Hang on Mum," replied Tom, "I was sitting at the front. I never even saw Big Bessie come in."

"That's true, I suppose" agreed mother, "but regardless, it's like your handiwork."

"Yeah" replied Tom, "like a real gangster, that's me."

It was meal time now. Just as Tom was getting his chair, there came a loud knock on the door. Tom being nearest went to open it. There stood Big Bessie.

"It's OK" she whispered, winking. "I've come to see your mum and dad" she said.

"Come in" invited Tom, "it's Auntie Bessie," he announced.

She came in, "Oh dear I'm sorry" she said, "I didn't t'ink about your meal time. I'll come back, begorrah so I will."

Tom winked at Kathy.

Mother said "Come in Bessie. Nice of you to drop in, would you like some lunch, there is plenty."

"No, mine's cooked at home you see, I only came in because Pastor Jones asked me to come and see you and to apologise if I upset you in any way."

"You haven't upset us" replied father. "Good old Bessie I say."

"And me" agreed mother.

"Me too" said Tom.

"What made you do it?" asked father.

"Well now, I listened to Pastor Jones and I've heard about the things she's been saying lately. I know her evil tongue was affecting you, my friends. I was that carried away as I listened to the sermon, so I threw her out."

"Well it's my little farmer's wife that got hurt" said Tom.

"Bless her" replied Big Bessie, coming over to shake her hand. "Well now," she said, "so you are the little coleen that goes to church each Sunday with Tom. I'm pleased to make your acquaintance, so I am. Now I must be on my way, I'll see you all again."

Off she went humming the tune of 'Danny Boy'.

As they ate their meal, Mr Monkton said "She's a character and no mistake."

"Auntie Gretchen" said Kathy, "please don't tell my mum about this."

"Of course not dear, no one will even give a hint."

That afternoon, as Kathy and Mrs Monkton went into the ward to see Mrs Eccles, they could see that she really was looking better now. She showed them how she could walk even without a stick.

"Next weekend" she told them, "I can go home."

"Now my dear, you just ring up, and father will come with the car to take you home."

Kathy told her all about the village fete, and how she won first prize for her fruit and almond cake, and how Tom won first prize in the fibber contest. This did cause a laugh. Then Kathy told her mum how Uncle Joe and Auntie Liz, said that she was most welcome at anytime.

"My, oh my," said Mrs Eccles, "you really have made some good friends. Gretchen I am eternally grateful to you for all you have done. You are indeed a true friend. As for Kathy, she just loves you."

"That's what friends are for" answered Gretchen.

At last it was time to go. Mrs Eccles promised to ring as soon as she knew the time of her release from hospital.

On the way home, Tom said, "We shall have to bike over to the farm tonight farmer's wife, because Dad isn't going over."

"I thought we all were," replied mother.

"So did I" agreed father.

"That's all I wanted to know then," replied Tom.

"You crafty old devil" said father.

"I know" replied Tom. "Now listen to this question then."

"Fire away," said father.

"Well in their natural state a pig lives in the forest, is that right?"

"Yes" agreed father.

"Well now" said Tom, "Uncle Joe has a three acre wood over there. Now why can't we pig wire it in; put pig huts in it, and let them roam about in there; say the old boar and so many dry sows?"

"Why did you have this in mind?" asked father.

"Easy," answered Tom, "it would cut down their food bills; they would be healthier; and you wouldn't need so much straw."

"Have you told Uncle Joe?"

"No" replied Tom.

"He probably never thought of it" said father, "I haven't myself. Yes it sounds a good idea, in any case for the summer."

"Well" continued Tom, "there is about six inches of dry leaves on the ground in the woods, they could make their own beds."

"Oh you lazy thing" said mother, "fancy making a poor little pig make its own bed."

"Sure, they don't have anything else to do" replied Tom, "so why not let them earn their keep? What do you say Dad?"

"Everytime a blood orange," answered father, "there is always so many other things to do, without waiting unnecessarily on pigs."

"I see," said mother, "like having an extra slice of cake and a mug of tea."

Tom had his leg pulled all the way home.

They took some things for Aunt Liz and set out for Bournend Farm. Uncle Joe was asleep in his chair, but he soon woke up as they arrived. They all went into the kitchen and sat down as Joe came toddling out to see them. Then mother and father related all that had happened to evil Kitty. Yes they both knew of Big Bessie, how they did laugh. Great Aunt Lizzie fair cried with laughter.

"So she called her evil Kitty, well I do declare, I've never heard the likes of it, what a jolly good name, evil Kitty."

Dear old Uncle Joe gave Tom a wink, which was seen by Kathy, then she knew that her mischievous Thomas was behind it all. Uncle Joe knew, she thought.

After a while Tom left for milking. "See you later" he said, "I've got the call of the wilds."

"I'm darned if you haven't" replied Joe laughing like a drain.

At last Tom had finished his jobs, all the animals were seen to. As he washed his hands, father came saying, "Uncle Joe and Aunt Liz needs you and your farmer's wife right now, so come on you two."

As they went in, Kathy whispered, "Are you in trouble Tom?"

"Whatever for?" he asked. "I can't think of anything."

So he took her hand and they went in. It was a biggish room that Uncle Joe used for his farm papers, maps, and the like. The same room had been used for this job ever since the first Monkton bought the farm.

"Everybody here now, Frank?" asked Great Uncle Joe.

"All present and correct" came the answer.

"Right then," said Uncle Joe, "I'm not very good at talking, so I shall only say this once, so please take notice all of you. Now

Aunt Liz and myself have made our wills, and we have decided to tell you all here and now ourselves, then there can be no mistakes. Now you are all affected by it, therefore we thought that if you knew you could start to work for yourselves from this day on; it's for your future after all. Mind you" he said, peering over his glasses, "one chap has already started doing that." Everyone looked at Tom. "Now father here, has agreed to start work on the old condemned cottage. After years of wrangling, I've managed to get my own way to do with it as I want. I want it altered, with two more downstairs rooms built on; it's for me and auntie for our retirement. You see we can't run upstairs anymore, and from this moment on should I die, Tom and his dear little farmer's wife, Kathy will inherit this farm. If I don't die, it's yours on your twenty-first birthday. We both look upon you two, as the son and daughter that we couldn't have."

"Oh Tom!" said Kathy holding tight to him.

He put his arm around her saying "Steady on old pet."

But she was just crying great tears of joy and happiness.

Aunt Liz came over and gave her a big handkerchief and tried to calm her down. "It's alright my dear we want you both to have it because you both love it so much, and we know it will be in good hands if a Monkton is here."

"Father here," continued Uncle Joe, "will inherit the farm cottage that he will be doing up. Should I die early, then father must be your overseer Tom, to help and advise you and to make it legal. He is the best one for that job. There will be money left for both father and Tom, but I don't know how much at this stage. But I will add there will be enough. Now Tom, this place will be yours, lock, stock and barrel. Tomorrow these papers will be put in the bank — Pastor Jones and Doctor James will execute the will — father will oversee for me. Any questions that may come to your minds, just come along and see me."

"I don't know of any right now," said Tom, "I'm just so happy and grateful."

Kathy could contain herself no longer, she just threw herself into Uncle Joe's arms, she kissed him saying, "I'm so happy I can't describe it Uncle. You and Auntie Liz have been so very sweet and nice to me. How can I ever thank you?"

"Don't try my dear. I didn't do it for thanks, I did it so that it would be in good hands. You see I know Master Thomas there, he makes a good job of everything even to getting his own back on evil Kitty for causing you so much trouble. How we have laughed over it this afternoon. You see my dear, it took a genius to think it all out like he did. He didn't want his friend, Pastor Jones to have to do a job that might have made him unpopular for himself among the townsfolk. So he had a talk with big Irish Bessie, nobody could have done it better. Nobody got hurt, and he knew of course that nobody in their right mind, would pick a row with Big Bessie, that's for sure. Oh no, we aren't cross with Tom, just very surprised at the darned clever way he did it. You see dear, I told Tom no punches on noses, that's what he wanted to do, natural I suppose. By the way Tom," said uncle, "father told me what you were thinking of doing in the woods down there. I must admit you have outstripped me. Yes, your thinking is very good. Now pig wire comes in fifty yard rolls, tell me how many you need, we shall definitely try out your idea."

Kathy still sat on uncle's knee. Everyone could see that uncle was pleased with her, because she showed that she liked him so much.

"Well that's about it for now," said uncle, "better have tea I suppose."

Off they all trooped to get their tea.

"I had to tell you Tom, I thought it best that you should know," said uncle, "then you can work for the future."

"My God, I will indeed," replied Tom.

As the family settled for tea, they all pulled Tom's leg about Big Bessie. "Yes" he told them "when I asked her to help, she said 'Suggest something'. After I had told her all of course. Then she said 'I've got it, begorrah and bejeepers, just you leave it to me boy'o. I'll be fixing it for evil Kitty, so I will, I'll t'ink of something now, so off ya' go and look after that little coleen.' Well I did just that, and lo and behold, she did do something."

"Well" replied mother, "I would never have agreed to it, if you had asked me."

"I know that" said Tom, "but a drastic situation needs drastic actions taken, it was very nasty for my farmer's wife you know. If we had allowed it to continue God only knows what would have happened."

"I wonder what she will do now?" asked mother.

"Not as much as you think" replied Tom.

"You sound as though it isn't finished yet then."

"Your guess is as good as mine," he replied.

Uncle Joe exchanged glances with Tom's father. Both men smiled and shook their heads.

After tea with the washing-up done, Tom was still talking to

Uncle Joe and father when Kathy came and sat with him.

"Fancy a little walk?" he asked. She agreed. "I'm off to pace out that wood" suggested Tom.

"Go in the bottom drawer of the office desk, there you will find a chain measure, use that, then you will have your measurements correct" suggested uncle.

Off they went hand-in-hand across the meadow to the wood, with the family watching them go from the window in sheer delight, glorying in their sweet young love.

When they got to the wood they found a ride going right through it, one side of the ride was quite small, the other side was much bigger.

"Tell you what" said Tom, "let's measure the small area first." It was 340 yards around it. "That's enough" he explained. "We'll try the pigs in this area first. Then if it works OK. We can wire in the big part. You see, if we wire it all in right away and it don't work too good, it becomes a waste of money and pig wire netting. I'll suggest to uncle, small bit first to experiment."

So they rolled up the chain measure, and wandered on down to the stream.

Suddenly a large dragon-fly swept past.

"Tom what was that, will it bite?"

"No" he said, "it's only a dragon-fly."

Back it came darting here and there, up and down they watched it go, then it settled on the flower heads of some meadowsweet.

Kathy crept near and was thrilled by its great beauty. "Look Tom," she whispered "it's so beautiful, it's absolutely gorgeous, could I keep one as a pet?"

"Not really" replied Tom, "I think dad said they only live for three days."

"Oh no!" exclaimed Kathy, "that's awfully sad."

"It's nature dear."

Then like a flash it darted away and was gone.

"It was gorgeous" she said.

Tom pointed out some trout, lying near the far bank; then they saw a large shoal of minnows near the place where the cows drank. Kathy watched them as they darted about, seemingly to play in the sun; then they saw a mother moorhen with her brood of chicks, she quickly called them to safety as they approached. Kathy was really thrilled with the wildlife of the stream.

They wandered on now back towards the farm. They could see the old flint-built farmhouse, and the apple orchard with its lovely crop of young apples decorating the branches. The farm buildings spread out before them. Tom saw that Kathy's eyes reflected her love for this peaceful old farm, nestling in the folds of the downs.

"Well my little farmer's wife," he said, "we know today what we must do all our lives. Farming is our game from now on. I have been teasing you about being a farmer's wife, now look how near it's got."

"Oh Tom, I felt so very happy, like all warm inside, all secure. I just had to cry, I really couldn't help it, I've made up my mind, I shall come and look after Uncle Joe and Auntie Liz as soon as I've finished school, and whenever I can leave Mum. It's the least I can do."

"Let me tell you, you will never regret it, or be out of pocket" replied Tom, "and by coming here you are really only coming home, because one day it will be your kitchen, your house."

"Yes Tom, and you will be working out on the farm, and I shall be so happy. Do you know Auntie Liz said that she would learn me all she knew about making butter, cream and cheese; and your mum has taught me lots about cooking. She can really cook nice Tom."

"I know" replied Tom, patting his belt.

Kathy smiled, "I reckon I've put some weight on since I've been with you. I've never been able to eat so well ever." Tom squeezed her hand and said, "It's your birthday in three weeks, we shall have a nice do then because your mum will be home."

"That's right, we can work something out. Leave it to me if you like" she told him.

They went indoors. The folks were talking and enjoying each other's company. Kathy told them about the big, big beautiful dragon-fly, the fish and the moorhen with her babies.

"It was so peaceful and lovely" she said, "I shall go again, that's for sure, to my friends, the fish and the birds."

Tom told uncle of what he had found out about the woods. "Now the small area to the left of the ride is only 340 yards around it. I thought if we tried that area first and it worked alright we could wire in the rest of the wood."

"I think it will work alright," replied uncle, "because you see, white pigs can get sunburned. I've never kept the black pigs so I can't vouch for them. By keeping the pigs in the woods, they would have the shade — it's cool in the summer and warmer in the winter. Yes I feel it's a winner, and so young Tom I will ring for seven rolls of pig wire tomorrow, then you can put it up as your time permits, and by the way we've got some portable pig huts. On skids they are, we can tow them down to the woods with the tractor."

"I suppose it would be wise to tow them in before we put up the wire," suggested Tom.

"Good thinking" replied uncle, "and by the way," he said, "we should really have a look at those huts to see if they need any repairs done to them before they go down to the woods. Mind you, Tom, we've only got about ten more days before we get cracking on the harvest job. Your dad will cut it with the old binder. We've got a Massey Harris, out in the barn with a six foot cut."

"Yes" said father, "we must go through that thoroughly together, and I'll explain how the knotter works and so on."

Tom was completely absorbed in all this talk of farming. Later that evening before he went to sleep, he did some writing, saying "Boy oh boy this should really do it."

The next morning he was up early, the first one down in fact. When mother came down, he was frying three well-pricked sausages and an egg for his breakfast.

"Goodness me," said mother, "you are up early."

"I thought I was late" replied Tom. "No wonder my farmer's wife isn't about."

While Tom ate his breakfast, Kathy came down followed by father.

"Hello!" he said, "somebody couldn't sleep I see."

"Slept like a log" replied Tom, chewing away.

"Then you didn't shave?" suggested father teasing.

"Look let me put you right on that point" replied Tom, "us farmers get so sunburned and our faces so red, that we just burn the stubble off. How can you hang about shaving, when you've got a dairy herd to milk like me, they must be seen to you know."

Father laughed at him, "A big herd of two 'eh?"

Tom gave Kathy and mum a quick kiss, then ran for his bike with his lunch bag that Kathy had put ready for him. He rode straight to the newspaper office building in the High Street. After pushing a letter through the editor's office door, he raced off to work. That evening as the folks in the High Street read their papers the front page carried an article which read as follows:—

'The Sanctuary has been cleansed'
Evil-tongued Kitty has been thrown out of the
church by the congregation, while the Minister preached
the facts of the ninth commandment.

Then there followed an account, no names were given. Father came in with an evening paper as the others were having their tea.

"Look at this mother," he said. "Now have you anything to do with this Thomas?"

"With what?" asked Tom. Then pretending to be nosey, he took the paper and read. "Blow me," he said, "and they have spelt commandment wrong." He handed back the paper saying "Big Bertha sure is in the news today."

"Don't be rude," replied Kathy. "What did it say?"

So mother handed her the paper to read the account for herself. When she finished she said, "It doesn't say that Big Be . . . that Auntie Bessie did it."

"Tom really, now you are getting Kathy all mixed up," said mother.

The youngsters studied their farming books, then Kathy had an idea. She started a big farm recipe book, of all the dishes she had learned to make.

Thursday evening rolled round. When Tom came home from work all the other members of the household were having their tea — Tom joined them. As they sat chatting, there came a knock on the door. Tom was nearest so he jumped up to answer it, he opened the door. There with her suitcase stood Mrs Eccles.

"Mum-in-law," he shouted, and he gave her a kiss and took her case saying, "Come on in. How did you get here?"

Up jumped the ladies, with Kathy embracing her dear old mum and crying with her happiness. Everyone made a great fuss. Tea was laid for her.

She told them how Doctor Harrington was coming to see Pastor Jones. "He came to the ward at three-thirty saying 'Come on I'm taking you home now,' so I couldn't let you know. He's just dropped me in the yard now. But I do have to take life steady for a while, no lifting, then I shall be OK."

Later that evening came another knock on the door. It was a lad who wanted to see Tom. His name was Harry Lucas, a high-spirited sort of lad. Tom had mentioned to him about evil Kitty and he ended by saying, "If I get news that she has left town, I'll give the bearer of that news five bob."

Now this is what he told Tom tonight. He said "I went to her house (as a joke you understand) with a note which I pinned to her door, it read:— 'Evil Kitty we are waiting to tar and feather you the very next time we see you out. Signed . . . The People.' Well I pinned it up like I said, and ran away sniggering to myself. Now today I rode by the house just in time to see a removal lorry leaving. It's empty you can go and see. On the removal lorry was Harris and Sons Removals and Storage, Bognor Regis; and that's five bob you owe me."

"You bet I do" replied Tom. But had no money on him, so he ran indoors and borrowed it off his dad. "Thanks Harry," he said "I'll see you around."

"What's all this about son?" asked father as Tom came back.

"Well" replied Tom, "come outside and I'll tell you."

So off out into the yard they went. Tom explained everything that had happened.

"Darned funny" said father, "they never turned up for work either."

Tom started to snigger, then they both howled with laughter.

"I bet old Uncle Joe will shake like a jelly when you tell him."

"Yeah," replied Tom, Aunt Liz will laugh until she does wet herself."

"You bet," howled father again.

They pulled themselves together and went indoors. Mrs Eccles had agreed with mother to stay in the flat with Kathy for tonight, then go home tomorrow. The bed where Kathy slept was a double bed, so all would be well.

"Have you told your mum about the farm?" whispered Tom to Kathy.

"No you tell her Tom."

"No" replied Tom, quite firmly, "you must take her in the sitting-room and tell her, because Dad and I want to tell Mum something, which I will tell you later."

"Alright then" agreed Kathy, off she went with her mother.

"Quick Dad, tell Mum they are gone in there for a minute."

So they told mother what had happened to Aunt Kitty.

"Oh you young devil" she said to Tom.

Then looking up at father's face, she started to howl and cry with great bursts of laughter.

"All I can say is," replied Tom, "it's good riddance to old rubbish, and God help the people of Bognor."

Poor old dad was really quite helpless now with laughter, all he could do was point at Tom.

"I think you had both better go over and tell them at the farm, and collect some fish and chips for supper at the same time," suggested mother.

So off went father and Tom to break the news.

When they arrived, Tom was to be the spokesman. He explained all that had happened to his great aunt and uncle. The old couple just fell about with laughter, it took them about ten minutes to pull themselves together. Aunt Liz had to go off in the end, but how pleased they were.

"That woman has been a pest" said uncle, "everytime I see her I think the same thing — there's that pest again."

Then father told of little Kathy's mother walking in at tea-time, having been brought home by the doctor who had come to see Pastor Jones.

"I wonder what that Kitty will do now?" asked auntie as she came back into the room.

"Have a shave suggested Tom."

"Have a shave?" said uncle, "how come?"

"Well" explained Tom, "one day a few years ago now, I was coming home from school; she stopped me and told me I was a disgrace. I looked at her and saw hair growing out of a small mole by her mouth, and I was very annoyed with her, so I said 'Why don't you go home and have a shave'. She swiped at me with her umbrella, missed and the handle came off. So I ran off home laughing at her."

This did the trick completely — oh how they laughed. This time poor old Aunt Liz did wet herself, she went quite helpless with laughter.

"Tom," said Uncle Joe drying his eyes, "you do make life worth living. I've never laughed so much in years, as I have done just lately."

"I know how you feel" said father.

Soon they had to leave to get fish and chips for supper.

"See you in the morning" shouted Tom.

Uncle Joe waved his stick still laughing, while poor old Aunt Liz was wiping her eyes saying "I'm sure I'm going to die."

"Oh, ha, ha, ha," and off they both went again laughing fit to burst.

That night at supper, Tom said, "How about a big celebration party on Kathy's birthday. We could celebrate her mum getting well — the exit of a certain person — to say nothing of the farm coming to us — the retiring farmer — oh yes and Kathy's birthday."

"Yes let's" agreed Kathy, "and we could ask Great Uncle Joe and Aunt Liz and Pastor Jones, because everyone has been so wonderful to me and Mum."

"Leave it to me" replied Mrs Monkton. "I'll let you know how I'm progressing."

"There you are farmer's wife," said Tom, "all cut and dried."

Mrs Eccles was always so amused by the two youngsters, and when she heard that the farm was left to them, she was overjoyed, and she just had to have a cry about it. Then in order to cheer them up, father told them of the time that Tom told his Auntie Kitty that she needed a shave, and that she took a swipe at him with her umbrella and the handle fell off.

Oh dear me, how they laughed at this mischievous Thomas.

The time went by quickly, Kathy and her mum went back to their own house, number six. How pleased she was to see it looking so very nice, so she said "This mum-in-law really does want to thank that farmer son-in-law, and his farmer's wife for doing such a wonderful job for me."

Eventually the great day came for the party. There was Kathy, and her mum, Great Uncle Joe and Great Aunt Elizabeth, Pastor Jones and his wife, mother, father, Tom, and Auntie Bessie. They really had a most enjoyable time.

Kathy said how thrilled she was that God had led her to find such wonderful friends. She thanked them all so much for their great kindness and friendship.

Mrs Eccles also thanked everyone, but could not find words to express herself, she just cried with her great happiness.

Uncle Joe said how happy, both he and Aunt Lizzie were to be able to leave the farm to a young Monkton, and his farmer's wife. Then uncle and aunt were clapped and cheered by all.

Pastor Jones said, how he delighted in knowing the family so well, and he hoped and prayed that their friendship would grow on into eternity. Then he said, "You know everyone, young Thomas once said to me, 'That despite all your preaching, the devil still sits among the congregation,' and looking back on my life, how right he seems to be. Mind you I may call on his services from time to time, in order to ferret that devil out. After all he does seem to be quite an expert."